THE STRANGE SCHEMES OF RANDOLPH MASON

By

Melville Davisson Post

INTRODUCTION.

THE teller of strange tales is not the least among benefactors of men. His cup of Lethe is welcome at times even to the strongest, when the *tædium vito* of the commonplace is in its meridian. To the aching victim of evil fortune, it is ofttimes the divine anaesthetic.

To-day a bitter critic calls down to the storyteller, bidding him turn out with the hewers of wood and the drawers of water, for the reason that there is no new thing, and the pieces with which he seeks to build are ancient and well worn. "At best," he cries, "the great one among you can produce but combinations of the old, some quaint, some monstrous, and all weary." But the writer does not turn out, and the world swings merrily on.

Perhaps the critic forgets that if things are old, men are new; that while the grain field stands fast, the waves passing over it are not one like the other. The new child is the best answer.

The reader is a clever tyrant. He demands something more than people of mist. There must be tendons in the ghost hand, and hard bones in the phantom, else he feels that he has been cheated.

Perhaps, of all things, the human mind loves best the problem. Not the problem of the abacus, but the problem of the chess-board when the pieces are living; the problem with passion and peril in it; with the fresh air of the hills and the salt breath of the sea. It propounds this riddle to the writer: Create mind-children, O Magician, with red blood in their faces, who, by power inherited from you, are enabled to secure the fruits of drudgery, without the drudgery. Nor must the genius of Circumstance help. Make them do what we cannot do, good Magician, but make them of clay as we are. We know all the old methods so well, and we are weary of them. Give us new ones.

Exacting is this taskmaster. It demands that the problem builder cunningly join together the Fancy and the Fact, and thereby enchant and bewilder, but not deceive. It demands all the mighty motives of life in the problem. Thus it happens that the toiler has tramped and retramped the field of crime. Poe and the French writers constructed masterpieces in the early day. Later came the flood of "Detective Stories" until the stomach of the reader failed. Yesterday, Mr. Conan Doyle created Sherlock Holmes, and the public pricked up its ears and listened with interest.

It is significant that the general plan of this kind of tale has never once been changed to any degree. The writers, one and all, have labored, often with great genius, to construct problems in crime, where by acute deduction the criminal and his methods were determined; or, reversing it, they have sought to plan the crime so cunningly as to effectually conceal the criminal and his methods. The intent has always been to baffle the trailer, and when the identity of the criminal was finally revealed, the story ended.

The high ground of the field of crime has not been explored; it has not even been entered. The book-stalls have been filled to weariness with tales based upon plans whereby the *detective*, or *ferreting* power of the State might be baffled. But, prodigious marvel! no writer has attempted to construct tales based upon plans whereby the *punishing* power of the State might be baffled.

The distinction, if one pauses for a moment to consider it, is striking. It is possible, even easy, deliberately to plan crimes so that the criminal agent and the criminal agency cannot be detected. Is it possible to plan and execute wrongs in such a manner that they will have all the effect and all the resulting profit of desperate crimes and yet not be crimes before the law?

There is, perhaps, nothing of which the layman is so grossly ignorant as of the law. He has grown to depend upon what he is pleased to call common sense. Indeed his refrain, "The law is common sense," has at times been echoed by the judiciary. There was never a graver error. The common sense of the common man is at best a poor guide to the criminal law. It is no guide at all to the civil law.

There is here no legal heresy. Lord Coke, in the seventeenth century, declared that the law was not the natural reason of man, and that men could not, out of their common reason, make such laws as the laws of England were. The laws have not grown simpler, surely, and if they could not be constructed by the common reason of men, they could certainly not be determined by it. That men have but indistinct ideas of the law is to be regretted and deplored. For their protection they should know it; and there is need of this protection. The voices of all men were not joined in the first great cry for law and order, nor are they all joined now. The hands of a part of mankind have ever been set against their fellows; for what great reason no man can tell. Maybe the Potter marred some, and certainly evil Circumstance marred some. But, by good hap, industry has always, and intelligence has usually, been on the law's side. Ofttimes, however, the Ishmælites raise up a genius and he, spying deep, sees the weak places in the law and the open holes in it, and forces through, to the great hurt of his fellows. And men standing in the market-places marvel.

We are prone to forget that the law is no perfect structure, that it is simply the result of human labor and human genius, and that whatever laws human ingenuity can create for the protection of men, those same laws human ingenuity can evade. The Spirit of Evil is no dwarf; he has developed equally with the Spirit of Good.

All wrongs are not crimes. Indeed only those wrongs are crimes in which certain technical elements are present. The law provides a Procrustean standard for all crimes. Thus a wrong, to become criminal, must fit exactly into the measure laid down by the law, else it is no crime; if it varies never so little from the legal measure, the law must, and will, refuse to regard it as criminal, no matter how injurious a wrong it may be. There is no measure of morality, or equity, or common right that can be applied to the individual case. The gauge of the law is iron-bound. The wrong measured by this gauge is either a crime or it is not. There is no middle ground.

Hence is it, that if one knows well the technicalities of the law, one may commit horrible wrongs that will yield all the gain and all the resulting effect of the highest crimes, and yet the wrongs perpetrated will constitute no one of the crimes described by the law. Thus the highest crimes, even murder, may be committed in such manner that although the criminal is known and the law holds him in custody, yet it cannot punish him. So it happens that in this year of our Lord of the nineteenth century, the skilful attorney marvels at the stupidity of the rogue who, committing crimes by the ordinary methods, subjects himself to unnecessary peril, when the result which he seeks can easily be attained by other methods, equally expeditious and without danger of liability in any criminal tribunal This is the field into which the author has ventured, and he believes it to be new and full of interest.

In order to develop these legal problems the author appreciated the need for a central figure. This central figure must of necessity be a lawyer of shrewdness and ability. Here a grave difficulty presented itself. No attorney, unless he were a superlative knave, could be presumed to suggest the committing of wrongs entailing grievous injury upon innocent men. On the other hand, no knave vicious enough to resort to such wrongs could be presumed to have learning enough to plan them, else he would not be driven to such straits. Hence the necessity for a character who should be without moral sense and yet should possess all the requisite legal acumen. Such a character is Randolph Mason, and while he may seem strange he is not impossible.

That great shocks and dread maladies may lop off a limb of the human mind and leave the other portions perfect, nay, may even wrench the human soul into one narrow groove, is the common lesson of the clinic and the mad-house. An intellect, keen, powerful, and yet devoid of any sense of moral obligation, would be no passing wonder to the skilled physician; for no one knows better than he that often in the house of the soul there are great chambers locked and barred and whole passages sealed up in the dark. Nor do men marvel that great minds concentrated on some mighty labor grow utterly oblivious to human relations and see and care for naught save the result which they are seeking. The chemist forgets that the diamond is precious, and burns it; the surgeon forgets that his patient is living and that the knife hurts as it cuts. Might not the great lawyer, striving tirelessly with the problems of men, come at last to see only the problem, with the people in it as pieces on a chess-board?

It may be objected that the writer has prepared here a text-book for the shrewd knave. To this it is answered that, if he instructs the enemies, he also warns the friends of law and order; and that Evil has never yet been stronger because the sun shone on it.

It should not be forgotten that this book deals with the law as it is and with no fanciful interpretation of it. The colors are woven into a gray warp of ancient and well settled legal principles, obtaining with full virtue in almost every state. The formula for every wrong in this book is as practical as the plan of an architect and may be played out by any skilful villain. Nor should it be presumed that the instances dealt with are exhaustive. The writer has presented but a few of the simpler and more conspicuous; there is, in truth, many another. Indeed the wonder grows upon him that the thief should stay up at night to steal.

Wheeling, W. Va., June 1, 1896.

I—THE CORPUS DELICTI

[See Lord Hale's Rule, Russell on Crimes. For the law in New York see 18th N. Y. Reports, 179; also N. Y. Reports, 49* page 137. The doctrine there laid down obtains in almost every State, with the possible exception of a few Western States, where the decisions are muddy.]

I.

THAT man Mason," said Samuel Walcott, "is the mysterious member of this club.

He is more than that; he is the mysterious man of New York."

"I was much surprised to see him," answered his companion, Marshall St. Clair, of the great law firm of Seward, St. Clair, & De Muth. "I had lost track of him since he went to Paris as counsel for the American stockholders of the Canal Company. When did he come back to the States?"

"He turned up suddenly in his ancient haunts about four months ago," said Walcott, "as grand, gloomy, and peculiar as Napoleon ever was in his palmiest days. The younger members of the club call him 'Zanona Redivivus'. He wanders through the house usually late at night, apparently without noticing anything or anybody. His mind seems to be deeply and busily at work, leaving his bodily self to wander as it may happen. Naturally, strange stories are told of him; indeed, his individuality and his habit of doing some unexpected thing, and doing it in such a marvellously original manner that men who are experts at it look on in wonder, cannot fail to make him an object of interest. He has never been known to play at any game whatever, and yet one night he sat down to the chess table with old Admiral Du Brey. You know the Admiral is the great champion since he beat the French and English officers in the tournament last winter. Well, you also know that the conventional openings at chess are scientifically and accurately determined. To the utter disgust of Du Brey, Mason opened the game with an unheard of attack from the extremes of the board. The old Admiral stopped and, in a kindly patronizing way, pointed out the weak and absurd folly of his move and asked him to begin again with some one of the safe openings. Mason smiled and answered that if one had a head that he could trust he should use it; if not, then it was the part of wisdom to follow blindly the dead forms of some man who had a head.

Du Brey was naturally angry and set himself to demolish Mason as quickly as possible. The game was rapid for a few moments. Mason lost piece after piece. His opening was broken and destroyed and its utter folly apparent to the lookers-on. The Admiral smiled and the game seemed all one-sided, when, suddenly, to his utter horror, Du Brey found that his king was in a trap. The foolish opening had been only a piece of shrewd strategy. The old Admiral fought and cursed and sacrificed his pieces, but it was of no use. He was gone. Mason checkmated him in two moves and arose wearily.

"'Where in Heaven's name, man,' said the old Admiral, thunderstruck, 'did you learn that masterpiece?'

"'Just here,' replied Mason. 'To play chess, one should know his opponent. How could the dead masters lay down rules by which you could be beaten, sir? They had never seen you'; and thereupon he turned and left the room. Of course, St. Clair, such a strange man would soon become an object of all kinds of mysterious rumors. Some are true and some are not. At any rate, I know that Mason is an unusual man with a gigantic intellect. Of late he seems to have taken a strange fancy to me. In fact, I seem to be the only member of the club that he will talk with, and I confess that he startles and fascinates me. He is an original genius, St. Clair, of an unusual order."

"I recall vividly," said the younger man, "that before Mason went to Paris he was considered one of the greatest lawyers of this city and he was feared and hated by the bar at large. He came here, I believe, from Virginia and began with the high-grade criminal practice. He soon became famous for his powerful and ingenious defences. He found holes in the law through which his clients escaped, holes that by the profession at large were not suspected to exist, and that frequently astonished the judges. His ability caught the attention of the great corporations. They tested him and found in him learning and unlimited resources. He pointed out methods by which they could evade obnoxious statutes, by which they could comply with the apparent letter of the law and yet violate its spirit, and advised them well in that most important of all things, just how far they could bend the law without breaking it. At the time he left for Paris he had a vast clientage and was in the midst of a brilliant career. The day he took passage from New York, the bar lost sight of him. No matter how great a man may be, the wave soon closes over him in a city like this. In a few years Mason was forgotten. Now only the older practitioners would recall him, and they would do so with hatred and bitterness. He was a tireless, savage, uncompromising fighter, always a recluse."

"Well," said Walcott, "he reminds me of a great world-weary cynic, transplanted from some ancient mysterious empire. When I come into the man's presence I feel instinctively the grip of his intellect. I tell you, St. Clair, Randolph Mason is the mysterious man of New York."

At this moment a messenger boy came into the room and handed Mr. Walcott a telegram. "St. Clair," said that gentleman, rising, "the directors of the Elevated are in session, and we must hurry."

The two men put on their coats and left the house.

Samuel Walcott was not a club man after the manner of the Smart Set, and yet he was in fact a club man. He was a bachelor in the latter thirties, and resided in a great silent house on the avenue. On the street he was a man of substance, shrewd and progressive, backed by great wealth. He had various corporate interests in the larger syndicates, but the basis and foundation of his fortune was real estate. His houses on the avenue were the best possible property, and his elevator row in the importers' quarter was indeed a literal gold mine. It was known that, many years before, his grandfather had died and left him the property, which, at that time, was of no great value. Young Walcott had gone out into the gold-fields and had been lost sight of and forgotten. Ten years afterward he had turned up suddenly in New York and taken possession of his property, then vastly increased in value. His speculations were almost phenomenally successful, and, backed by the now enormous value of his real property, he was soon on a level with the merchant princes. His judgment was considered sound, and he had the full confidence of his business associates for safety and caution. Fortune heaped up riches around him with a lavish hand. He was unmarried and the halo of his wealth caught the keen eye of the matron with marriageable daughters. He was invited out, caught by the whirl of society, and tossed into its maelstrom. In a measure he reciprocated. He kept horses and a yacht. His dinners at Delmonico's and the club were above reproach. But with all he was a silent man with a shadow deep in his eyes, and seemed to court the society of his fellows, not because he loved them, but because he either hated or feared solitude. For years the strategy of the match-maker had gone gracefully afield, but Fate is relentless. If she shields the victim from the traps of men, it is not because she wishes him to escape, but because she is pleased to reserve him for her own trap. So it happened that, when Virginia St. Clair assisted Mrs. Miriam Steuvisant at her midwinter reception, this same Samuel Walcott fell deeply and hopelessly and utterly in love, and it was so apparent to the beaten generals present, that Mrs. Miriam Steuvisant applauded herself, so to speak, with encore after encore. It was good to see this courteous, silent man literally at the feet of the young debutante. He was there of right. Even the mothers of marriageable daughters admitted that. The young girl was brown-haired, brown-eyed, and tall enough, said the experts, and of the blue blood royal, with all the grace, courtesy, and inbred genius of such princely heritage.

Perhaps it was objected by the censors of the Smart Set that Miss St. Clair's frankness and honesty were a trifle old-fashioned, and that she was a shadowy bit of a Puritan; and perhaps it was of these same qualities that Samuel Walcott received his hurt. At any rate the hurt was there and deep, and the new actor stepped up into the old time-worn, semi-tragic drama, and began his rôle with a tireless, utter sincerity that was deadly dangerous if he lost.

II

Perhaps a week after the conversation between St. Clair and Walcott, Randolph Mason stood in the private writing-room of the club with his hands behind his back.

He was a man apparently in the middle forties; tall and reasonably broad across the shoulders; muscular without being either stout or lean. His hair was thin and of a brown color, with erratic streaks of gray. His forehead was broad and high and of a faint reddish color. His eyes were restless inky black, and not over-large. The nose was big and muscular and bowed. The eyebrows were black and heavy, almost bushy. There were heavy furrows, running from the nose downward and outward to the corners of the mouth. The mouth was straight and the jaw was heavy, and square.

Looking at the face of Randolph Mason from above, the expression in repose was crafty and cynical; viewed from below upward, it was savage and vindictive, almost brutal; while from the front, if looked squarely in the face, the stranger was fascinated by the animation of the man and at once concluded that his expression was fearless and sneering. He was evidently of Southern extraction and a man of unusual power.

A fire smouldered on the hearth. It was a crisp evening in the early fall, and with that far-off touch of melancholy which ever heralds the coming winter, even in the midst of a city. The man's face looked tired and ugly. His long white hands were clasped tight together. His entire figure and face wore every mark of weakness and physical exhaustion; but his eyes contradicted. They were red and restless.

In the private dining-room the dinner party was in the best of spirits. Samuel Walcott was happy. Across the table from him was Miss Virginia St. Clair, radiant, a tinge of color in her cheeks. On either side, Mrs. Miriam Steuvisant and Marshall St. Clair were brilliant and light-hearted. Walcott looked at the young girl and the measure of his worship was full. He wondered for the thousandth time how she could possibly love him and by what earthly miracle she had come to accept him, and how it would be always to have her across the table from him, his own table in his own house.

They were about to rise from the table when one of the waiters entered the room and handed Walcott an envelope. He thrust it quickly into his pocket In the confusion of rising the others did not notice him, but his face was ash-white and his hands trembled violently as he placed the wraps around the bewitching shoulders of Miss St. Clair.

"Marshall," he said, and despite the powerful effort his voice was hollow, "you will see the ladies safely cared for, I am called to attend a grave matter."

"All right, Walcott," answered the young man, with cheery good-nature, "you are too serious, old man, trot along."

"The poor dear," murmured Mrs. Steuvisant, after Walcott had helped them to the carriage and turned to go up the steps of the club,—"The poor dear is hard hit, and men are such funny creatures when they are hard hit."

Samuel Walcott, as his fate would, went direct to the private writing-room and opened the door. The lights were not turned on and in the dark he did not see Mason motionless by the mantel-shelf. He went quickly across the room to the writing-table, turned on one of the lights, and, taking the envelope from his pocket, tore it open. Then he bent down by the light to read the contents. As his eyes ran over the paper, his jaw fell. The skin drew away from his cheek-bones and his face seemed literally to sink in. His knees gave way under him and he would have gone down in a heap had it not been for Mason's long arms that closed around him and held him up. The human economy is ever mysterious. The moment the new danger threatened, the latent power of the man as an animal, hidden away in the centres of intelligence, asserted itself. His hand clutched the paper and, with a half slide, he turned in Mason's arms. For a moment he stared up at the ugly man whose thin arms felt like wire ropes.

"You are under the dead-fall, aye," said Mason. "The cunning of my enemy is sublime."

"Your enemy?" gasped Walcott. "When did you come into it? How in

God's name did you know it? How your enemy?"

Mason looked down at the wide bulging eyes of the man.

"Who should know better than I?" he said. "Haven't I broken through all the traps and plots that she could set?"

"She? She trap you?" The man's voice was full of horror.

"The old schemer," muttered Mason. "The cowardly old schemer, to strike in the back; but we can beat her. She did not count on my helping you—I, who know her so well."

Mason's face was red, and his eyes burned. In the midst of it all he dropped his hands and went over to the fire. Samuel Walcott arose, panting, and stood looking at Mason, with his hands behind him on the table. The naturally strong nature and the rigid school in which the man had been trained presently began to tell. His composure in part returned and he thought rapidly. What did this strange man know? Was he simply making shrewd guesses, or had he some mysterious knowledge of this matter? Walcott could not know that Mason meant only Fate, that he believed her to be his great enemy. Walcott had never before doubted his own ability to meet any emergency. This mighty jerk had carried him off his feet. He was unstrung and panic-stricken. At any rate this man had promised help. He would take it. He put the paper and envelope carefully into his pocket, smoothed out his rumpled coat, and going over to Mason touched him on the shoulder.

"Come," he said, "if you are to help me we must go."

The man turned and followed him without a word. In the hall Mason put on his hat and overcoat, and the two went out into the street. Walcott hailed a cab, and the two were driven to his house on the avenue. Walcott took out his latch-key, opened the door, and led the way into the library. He turned on the light and motioned Mason to seat himself at the table. Then he went into another room and presently returned with a bundle of papers and a decanter of brandy. He poured out a glass of the liquor and offered it to Mason. The man shook his head. Walcott poured the contents of the glass down his own throat. Then he set the decanter down and drew up a chair on the side of the table opposite Mason.

"Sir," said Walcott, in a voice deliberate, indeed, but as hollow as a sepulchre, "I am done for. God has finally gathered up the ends of the net, and it is knotted tight."

"Am I not here to help you?" said Mason, turning savagely. "I can beat Fate. Give me the details of her trap."

He bent forward and rested his arms on the table. His streaked gray hair was rumpled and on end, and his face was ugly. For a moment Walcott did not answer. He moved a little into the shadow; then he spread the bundle of old yellow papers out before him.

"To begin with," he said, "I am a living lie, a gilded crime-made sham, every bit of me. There is not an honest piece anywhere. It is all lie. I am a liar and a thief before men. The property which I possess is not mine, but stolen from a dead man. The very name which I bear is not my own, but is the bastard child of a crime. I am more than all that—I am a murderer; a murderer before the law; a murderer before God; and worse than a murderer before the pure woman whom I love more than anything that God could make."

He paused for a moment and wiped the perspiration from his face.

"Sir," said Mason, "this is all drivel, infantile drivel. What you are is of no importance. How to get out is the problem, how to get out."

Samuel Walcott leaned forward, poured out a glass of brandy and swallowed it.

"Well," he said, speaking slowly, "my right name is Richard Warren. In the spring of 1879 I came to New York and fell in with the real Samuel Walcott, a young man with a little money and some property which his grandfather had left him. We became friends, and concluded to go to the far west together. Accordingly we scraped together what money we could lay our hands on, and landed in the gold-mining regions of

California. We were young and inexperienced, and our money went rapidly. One April morning we drifted into a little shack camp, away up in the Sierra Nevadas, called Hell's Elbow. Here we struggled and starved for perhaps a year. Finally, in utter desperation, Walcott married the daughter of a Mexican gambler, who ran an eating-house and a poker joint. With them we lived from hand to mouth in a wild God-forsaken way for several years. After a time the woman began to take a strange fancy to me. Walcott finally noticed it, and grew jealous.

"One night, in a drunken brawl, we quarrelled, and I killed him. It was late at night, and, beside the woman, there were four of us in the poker room,—the Mexican gambler, a half-breed devil called Cherubim Pete, Walcott, and myself. When Walcott fell, the half-breed whipped out his weapon, and fired at me across the table; but the woman, Nina San Croix, struck his arm, and, instead of killing me, as he intended, the bullet mortally wounded her father, the Mexican gambler. I shot the half-breed through the forehead, and turned round, expecting the woman to attack me. On the contrary, she pointed to the window, and bade me wait for her on the cross-trail below.

"It was fully three hours later before the woman joined me at the place indicated. She had a bag of gold dust, a few jewels that belonged to her father, and a package of papers. I asked her why she had stayed behind so long, and she replied that the men were not killed outright, and that she had brought a priest to them and waited until they had died. This was the truth, but not all the truth. Moved by superstition or foresight, the woman had induced the priest to take down the sworn statements of the two dying men, seal it, and give it to her. This paper she brought with her. All this I learned afterwards. At the time I knew nothing of this damning evidence.

"We struck out together for the Pacific coast. The country was lawless. The privations we endured were almost past belief. At times the woman exhibited cunning and ability that were almost genius; and through it all, often in the very fingers of death, her devotion to me never wavered. It was dog-like, and seemed to be her only object on earth. When we reached San Francisco, the woman put these papers into my hands."

Walcott took up the yellow package, and pushed it across the table to Mason.

"She proposed that I assume Walcott's name, and that we come boldly to New York and claim the property. I examined the papers, found a copy of the will by which Walcott inherited the property, a bundle of correspondence, and sufficient documentary evidence to establish his identity beyond the shadow of a doubt. Desperate gambler as I now was, I quailed before the daring plan of Nina San Croix. I urged that I, Richard Warren, would be known, that the attempted fraud would be detected and would result in investigation, and perhaps unearth the whole horrible matter.

"The woman pointed out how much I resembled Walcott, what vast changes ten years of such life as we had led would naturally be expected to make in men, how utterly impossible it would be to trace back the fraud to Walcott's murder at Hell's Elbow, in the wild passes of the Sierra Nevadas. She bade me remember that we were both outcasts, both crime-branded, both enemies of man's law and God's; that we had nothing to lose; we were both sunk to the bottom. Then she laughed, and said that she had not found me a coward until now, but that if I had turned chicken-hearted, that was the end of it, of course. The result was, we sold the gold dust and jewels in San Francisco, took on such evidences of civilization as possible, and purchased passage to New York on the best steamer we could find.

"I was growing to depend on the bold gambler spirit of this woman, Nina San Croix; I felt the need of her strong, profligate nature. She was of a queer breed and a queerer school. Her mother was the daughter of a Spanish engineer, and had been stolen by the Mexican, her father. She herself had been raised and educated as best might be in one of the monasteries along the Rio Grande, and had there grown to womanhood before her father, fleeing into the mountains of California, carried her with him.

"When we landed in New York I offered to announce her as my wife, but she refused, saying that her presence would excite comment and perhaps attract the attention of Walcott's relatives. We therefore arranged that I should go alone into the city, claim the property, and announce myself as Samuel Walcott, and that she should remain under cover until such time as we would feel the ground safe under us.

"Every detail of the plan was fatally successful. I established my identity without difficulty and secured the property. It had increased vastly in value, and I, as Samuel Walcott, soon found myself a rich man. I went to Nina San Croix in hiding and gave her a large sum of money, with which she purchased a residence in a retired part of the city, far up in the northern suburb. Here she lived secluded and unknown while I remained in the city, living here as a wealthy bachelor.

"I did not attempt to abandon the woman, but went to her from time to time in disguise and under cover of the greatest secrecy. For a time everything ran smooth, the woman was still devoted to me above everything else, and thought always of my welfare first and seemed content to wait so long as I thought best. My business expanded. I was sought after and consulted and drawn into the higher life of New York, and more and more felt that the woman was an albatross on my neck. I put her off with one excuse after another. Finally she began to suspect me and demanded that I should recognize her as my wife. I attempted to point out the difficulties. She met them all by saying that we should both go to Spain, there I could marry her and we could return to America and drop into my place in society without causing more than a passing comment.

"I concluded to meet the matter squarely once for all. I said that I would convert half of the property into money and give it to her, but that I would not marry her. She did not fly into a storming rage as I had expected, but went quietly out of the room and presently returned with two papers, which she read. One was the certificate of her marriage to Walcott duly authenticated; the other was the dying statement of her father, the Mexican gambler, and of Samuel Walcott, charging me with murder. It was in proper form and certified by the Jesuit priest.

"Now," she said, sweetly, when she had finished, 'which do you prefer, to recognize your wife, or to turn all the property over to Samuel Walcott's widow and hang for his murder?'

"I was dumbfounded and horrified. I saw the trap that I was in and I consented to do anything she should say if she would only destroy the papers. This she refused to do. I pleaded with her and implored her to destroy them. Finally she gave them to me with a great show of returning confidence, and I tore them into bits and threw them into the fire.

"That was three months ago. We arranged to go to Spain and do as she said. She was to sail this morning and I was to follow. Of course I never intended to go. I congratulated myself on the fact that all trace of evidence against me was destroyed and that her grip was now broken. My plan was to induce her to sail, believing that I would follow. When she was gone I would marry Miss St. Clair, and if Nina San Croix should return I would defy her and lock her up as a lunatic. But I was reckoning like an infernal ass, to imagine for a moment that I could thus hoodwink such a woman as Nina San Croix.

"To-night I received this." Walcott took the envelope from his pocket and gave it to Mason. "You saw the effect of it; read it and you will understand why. I felt the death hand when I saw her writing on the envelope."

Mason took the paper from the envelope. It was written in Spanish, and ran:

"Greeting to Richard Warren.

"The great Senor does his little Nina injustice to think she would go away to Spain and leave him to the beautiful American. She is not so thoughtless. Before she goes, she shall be, Oh so very rich! and the dear Senor shall be, Oh so very safe! The Archbishop and the kind Church hate murderers.

"Nina San Croix.

"Of course, fool, the papers you destroyed were copies.

"N. San C."

To this was pinned a line in a delicate aristocratic hand, saying that the Archbishop would willingly listen to Madam San Croix's statement if she would come to him on Friday morning at eleven.

"You see," said Walcott, desperately, "there is no possible way out. I know the woman—when she decides to do a thing that is the end of it. She has decided to do this."

Mason turned around from the table, stretched out his long legs, and thrust his hands deep into his pockets. Walcott sat with his head down, watching Mason hopelessly, almost indifferently, his face blank and sunken. The ticking of the bronze clock on the mantel-shelf was loud, painfully loud. Suddenly Mason drew his knees in and bent over, put both his bony hands on the table, and looked at Walcott.

"Sir," he said, "this matter is in such shape that there is only one thing to do. This growth must be cut out at the roots, and cut out quickly. This is the first fact to be determined, and a fool would know it. The second fact is that you must do it yourself. Hired killers are like the grave and the daughters of the horse-leech,—they cry always, 'Give, Give,' They are only palliatives, not cures. By using them you swap perils. You simply take a stay of execution at best. The common criminal would know this. These are the facts of your problem. The master plotters of crime would see here but two difficulties to meet:

"A practical method for accomplishing the body of the crime.

"A cover for the criminal agent.

"They would see no farther, and attempt to guard no farther. After they had provided a plan for the killing, and a means by which the killer could cover his trail and escape from the theatre of the homicide, they would believe all the requirements of the problems met, and would stop. The greatest, the very giants among them, have stopped here and have been in great error.

"In every crime, especially in the great ones, there exists a third element, pre-eminently vital. This third element the master plotters have either overlooked or else have not had the genius to construct. They plan with rare cunning to baffle the victim. They plan with vast wisdom, almost genius, to baffle the trailer. But they fail utterly to provide any plan for baffling the punisher. Ergo, their plots are fatally defective and often result in ruin. Hence the vital necessity for providing the third element— the *escape ipso jure*."

Mason arose, walked around the table, and put his hand firmly on Samuel Walcott's shoulder. "This must be done to-morrow night," he continued; "you must arrange your business matters to-morrow and announce that you are going on a yacht cruise, by order of your physician, and may not return for some weeks. You must prepare your yacht for a voyage, instruct your men to touch at a certain point on Staten Island, and wait until six o'clock day after to-morrow morning. If you do not come aboard by that time, they are to go to one of the South American ports and remain until further orders. By this means your absence for an indefinite period will be explained. You will go to Nina San Croix in the disguise which you have always used, and from her to the yacht, and by this means step out of your real status and back into it without leaving traces. I will come here to-morrow evening and furnish you with everything that you shall need and give you full and exact instructions in every particular. These details you must execute with the greatest care, as they will be vitally essential to the success of my plan."

Through it all Walcott had been silent and motionless. Now he arose, and in his face there must have been some premonition of protest, for Mason stepped back and put out his hand. "Sir," he said, with brutal emphasis, "not a word. Remember that you are only the hand, and the hand does not think." Then he turned around abruptly and went out of the house.

III.

The place which Samuel Walcott had selected for the residence of Nina San Croix was far up in the northern suburb of New York. The place was very old. The lawn was large and ill-kept; the house, a square old-fashioned brick, was set far back from the street, and partly hidden by trees. Around it all was a rusty iron fence. The place had the air of genteel ruin, such as one finds in the Virginias.

On a Thursday of November, about three o'clock in the afternoon, a little man, driving a dray, stopped in the alley at the rear of the house. As he opened the back gate an old negro woman came down the steps from the kitchen and demanded to know what he wanted. The drayman asked if the lady of the house was in. The old negro answered that she was asleep at this hour and could not be seen.

"That is good," said the little man, "now there won't be any row. I brought up some cases of wine which she ordered from our house last week and which the Boss told me to deliver at once, but I forgot it until to-day. Just let me put it in the cellar now, Auntie, and don't say a word to the lady about it and she won't ever know that it was not brought up on time."

The drayman stopped, fished a silver dollar out of his pocket, and gave it to the old negro. "There now, Auntie," he said, "my job depends upon the lady not knowing about this wine; keep it mum."

"Dat's all right, honey," said the old servant, beaming like a May morning. "De cellar door is open, carry it all in and put it in de back part and nobody aint never going to know how long it has been in 'dar."

The old negro went back into the kitchen and the little man began to unload the dray. He carried in five wine cases and stowed them away in the back part of the cellar as the old woman had directed. Then, after having satisfied himself that no one was watching, he took from the dray two heavy paper sacks, presumably filled with flour, and a little bundle wrapped in an old newspaper; these he carefully hid behind the wine cases in the cellar. After a while he closed the door, climbed on his dray, and drove off down the alley.

About eight o'clock in the evening of the same day, a Mexican sailor dodged in the front gate and slipped down to the side of the house. He stopped by the window and tapped on it with his finger. In a moment a woman opened the door. She was tall, lithe, and splendidly proportioned, with a dark Spanish face and straight hair. The man stepped inside. The woman bolted the door and turned round.

"Ah," she said, smiling, "it is you, Senor? How good of you."

The man started. "Whom else did you expect?" he said quickly.

"Oh!" laughed the woman, "perhaps the Archbishop."

"Nina!" said the man, in a broken voice that expressed love, humility, and reproach. His face was white under the black sunburn.

For a moment the woman wavered. A shadow flitted over her eyes, then she stepped back. "No," she said, "not yet."

The man walked across to the fire, sank down in a chair, and covered his face with his hands. The woman stepped up noiselessly behind him and leaned over the chair. The man was either in great agony or else he was a superb actor, for the muscles of his neck twitched violently and his shoulders trembled.

"Oh," he muttered, as though echoing his thoughts, "I can't do it, I can't!"

The woman caught the words and leaped up as though some one had struck her in the face. She threw back her head. Her nostrils dilated and her eyes flashed.

"You can't do it!" she cried. "Then you do love her! You shall do it! Do you hear me? You shall do it! You killed him! You got rid of him! but you shall not get rid of me. I have the evidence, all of it. The Archbishop will have it to-morrow. They shall hang you! Do you hear me? They shall hang you!"

The woman's voice rose, it was loud and shrill. The man turned slowly round without looking up, and stretched out his arms toward the woman. She stopped and looked down at him. The fire glittered for a moment and then died out of her eyes, her bosom heaved and her lips began to tremble. With a cry she flung herself into his arms, caught him around the neck, and pressed his face up close against her cheek.

"Oh! Dick, Dick," she sobbed, "I do love you so! I can't live without you! Not another hour Dick! I do want you so much, so much, Dick!" The man shifted his right arm quickly, slipped a great Mexican knife out of his sleeve, and passed his fingers slowly up the woman's side until he felt the heart beat under his hand, then he raised the knife, gripped the handle tight, and drove the keen blade into the woman's bosom. The hot blood gushed out over his arm, and down on his leg. The body, warm and limp, slipped down in his arms. The man got up, pulled out the knife, and thrust it into a sheath at his belt, unbuttoned the dress, and slipped it off of the body. As he did this a bundle of papers dropped upon the floor; these he glanced at hastily and put into his pocket. Then he took the dead woman up in his arms, went out into the hall, and started to go up the stairway. The body was relaxed and heavy, and for that reason difficult to carry. He doubled it up into an awful heap, with the knees against the chin, and walked slowly and heavily up the stairs and out into the bath-room. There he laid the corpse down on the tiled floor. Then he opened the window, closed the shutters, and lighted the gas. The bath-room was small and contained an ordinary steel tub, porcelain-lined, standing near the window and raised about six inches above the floor. The sailor went over to the tub, pried up the metal rim of the outlet with his knife, removed it, and fitted into its place a porcelain disk which he took from his pocket; to this disk was attached a long platinum wire, the end of which he fastened on the outside of the tub. After he had done this he went back to the body, stripped off its clothing, put it down in the tub and began to dismember it with the great Mexican knife. The blade was strong and sharp as a razor. The man worked rapidly and with the greatest care.

When he had finally cut the body into as small pieces as possible, he replaced the knife in its sheath, washed his hands, and went out of the bath-room and down stairs to the lower hall. The sailor seemed perfectly familiar with the house. By a side door he passed into the cellar. There he lighted the gas, opened one of the wine cases, and, taking up all the bottles that he could conveniently carry, returned to the bath-room. There he poured the contents into the tub on the dismembered body, and then returned to the cellar with the empty bottles, which he replaced in the wine cases. This he continued to do until all the cases but one were emptied and the bath tub was more than half full of liquid. This liquid was sulphuric acid.

When the sailor returned to the cellar with the last empty wine bottles, he opened the fifth case, which really contained wine, took some of it out, and poured a little into each of the empty bottles in order to remove any possible odor of the sulphuric acid. Then he turned out the gas and brought up to the bath-room with him the two paper flour sacks and the little heavy bundle. These sacks were filled with nitrate of soda. He set them down by the door, opened the little bundle, and took out two long rubber tubes, each attached to a heavy gas burner, not unlike the ordinary burners of a small gas-stove. He fastened the tubes to two of the gas jets, put the burners under the tub, turned the gas on full, and lighted it. Then he threw into the tub the woman's clothing and the papers which he had found on her body, after which he took up the two heavy sacks of nitrate of soda and dropped them carefully into the sulphuric acid. When he had done this he went quickly out of the bath-room and closed the door.

The deadly acids at once attacked the body and began to destroy it; as the heat increased, the acids boiled and the destructive process was rapid and awful. From time to time the sailor opened the door of the bath-room cautiously, and, holding a wet towel over his mouth and nose, looked in at his horrible work. At the end of a few hours there was only a swimming mass in the tub. When the man looked at four o'clock, it was all a thick murky liquid. He turned off the gas quickly and stepped back out of the room. For perhaps half an hour he waited in the hall; finally, when the acids had cooled so that they no longer gave off fumes, he opened the door and went in, took hold of the platinum wire and, pulling the porcelain disk from the stop-cock, allowed the awful contents of the tub to run out. Then he turned on the hot water, rinsed the tub clean, and replaced the metal outlet. Removing the rubber tubes, he cut them into pieces, broke the porcelain disk, and, rolling up the platinum wire, washed it all down the sewer pipe.

The fumes had escaped through the open window; this he now closed and set himself to putting the bath-room in order, and effectually removing every trace of his night's work. The sailor moved around with the very greatest degree of care. Finally, when he had arranged everything to his complete satisfaction, he picked up the two burners, turned out the gas, and left the bath-room, closing the door after him. From the bath-room he went directly to the attic, concealed the two rusty burners under a heap of rubbish, and then walked carefully and noiselessly down the stairs and through the lower hall. As he opened the door and stepped into the room where he had killed the woman, two police-officers sprang out and seized him. The man screamed like a wild beast taken in a trap and sank down.

"Oh! oh!" he cried, "it was no use! it was no use to do it!" Then he recovered himself in a manner and was silent. The officers handcuffed him, summoned the patrol, and took him at once to the station-house. There he said he was a Mexican sailor and that his name was Victor Ancona; but he would say nothing further. The following morning he sent for Randolph Mason and the two were long together.

IV.

The obscure defendant charged with murder has little reason to complain of the law's delays. The morning following the arrest of Victor Ancona, the newspapers published long sensational articles, denounced him as a fiend, and convicted him. The grand jury, as it happened, was in session. The preliminaries were soon arranged and the case was railroaded into trial. The indictment contained a great many counts, and charged the prisoner with the murder of Nina San Croix by striking, stabbing, choking, poisoning, and so forth.

The trial had continued for three days and had appeared so overwhelmingly one-sided that the spectators who were crowded in the court-room had grown to be violent and bitter partisans, to such an extent that the police watched them closely. The attorneys for the People were dramatic and denunciatory, and forced their case with arrogant confidence. Mason, as counsel for the prisoner, was indifferent and listless. Throughout the entire trial he had sat almost motionless at the table, his gaunt form bent over, his long legs drawn up under his chair, and his weary, heavy-muscled face, with its restless eyes, fixed and staring out over the heads of the jury, was like a tragic mask. The bar, and even the judge, believed that the prisoner's counsel had abandoned his case.

The evidence was all in and the People rested. It had been shown that Nina San Croix had resided for many years in the house in which the prisoner was arrested; that she had lived by herself, with no other companion than an old negro servant; that her past was unknown, and that she received no visitors, save the Mexican sailor, who came to her house at long intervals. Nothing whatever was shown tending to explain who the prisoner was or whence he had come. It was shown that on Tuesday preceding the killing the Archbishop had received a communication from Nina San Croix, in which she said she desired to make a statement of the greatest import, and asking for an audience. To this the Archbishop replied that he would willingly grant her a hearing if she would come to him at eleven o'clock on Friday morning. Two policemen testified that about eight o'clock on the night of Thursday they had noticed the prisoner slip into the gate of Nina San Croix's residence and go down to the side of the house, where he was admitted; that his appearance and seeming haste had attracted their attention; that they had concluded that it was some clandestine amour, and out of curiosity had both slipped down to the house and endeavored to find a position from which they could see into the room, but were unable to do so, and were about to go back to the street when they heard a woman's voice cry out in great anger: "I know that you love her and that you want to get rid of me, but you shall not do it! You murdered him, but you shall not murder me!

I have all the evidence to convict you of murdering him! The Archbishop will have it to-morrow! They shall hang you! Do you hear me? They shall hang you for his murder!" that thereupon one of the policemen proposed that they should break into the house and see what was wrong, but the other had urged that it was only the usual lovers' quarrel and if they should interfere they would find nothing upon which a charge could be based and would only be laughed at by the chief; that they had waited and listened for a time, but hearing nothing further had gone back to the street and contented themselves with keeping a strict watch on the house.

The People proved further, that on Thursday evening Nina San Croix had given the old negro domestic a sum of money and dismissed her, with the instruction that she was not to return until sent for. The old woman testified that she had gone directly to the house of her son, and later had discovered that she had forgotten some articles of clothing which she needed; that thereupon she had returned to the house and had gone up the back way to her room,—this was about eight o'clock; that while there she had heard Nina San Croix's voice in great passion and remembered that she had used the words stated by the policemen; that these sudden, violent cries had frightened her greatly and she had bolted the door and been afraid to leave the room; shortly thereafter, she had heard heavy footsteps ascending the stairs, slowly and with great difficulty, as though some one were carrying a heavy burden; that therefore her fear had increased and that she had put out the light and hidden under the bed. She remembered hearing the footsteps moving about up-stairs for many hours, how long she could not tell Finally, about half-past four in the morning, she crept out, opened the door, slipped down stairs, and ran out into the street. There she had found the policemen and requested them to search the house.

The two officers had gone to the house with the woman. She had opened the door and they had had just time to step back into the shadow when the prisoner entered. When arrested, Victor Ancona had screamed with terror, and cried out, "It was no use! it was no use to do it!"

The Chief of Police had come to the house and instituted a careful search. In the room below, from which the cries had come, he found a dress which was identified as belonging to Nina San Croix and which she was wearing when last seen by the domestic, about six o'clock that evening. This dress was covered with blood, and had a slit about two inches long in the left side of the bosom, into which the Mexican knife, found on the prisoner, fitted perfectly. These articles were introduced in evidence, and it was shown that the slit would be exactly over the heart of the wearer, and that such a wound would certainly result in death. There was much blood on one of the chairs and on the floor. There was also blood on the prisoner's coat and the leg of his trousers, and the heavy Mexican knife was also bloody. The blood was shown by the experts to be human blood.

The body of the woman was not found, and the most rigid and tireless search failed to develop the slightest trace of the corpse, or the manner of its disposal. The body of the woman had disappeared as completely as though it had vanished into the air.

When counsel announced that he had closed for the People, the judge turned and looked gravely down at Mason. "Sir," he said, "the evidence for the defence may now be introduced."

Randolph Mason arose slowly and faced the judge.

"If your Honor please," he said, speaking slowly and distinctly, "the defendant has no evidence to offer." He paused while a murmur of astonishment ran over the court-room. "But, if your Honor please," he continued, "I move that the jury be directed to find the prisoner not guilty."

The crowd stirred. The counsel for the People smiled. The judge looked sharply at the speaker over his glasses. "On what ground?" he said curtly.

"On the ground," replied Mason, "that the *corpus delicti* has not been proven."

"Ah!" said the judge, for once losing his judicial gravity.

Mason sat down abruptly. The senior counsel for the prosecution was on his feet in a moment.

"What!" he said, "the gentleman bases his motion on a failure to establish the *corpus delicti?* Does he jest, or has he forgotten the evidence? The term '*corpus delicti*' is technical, and means the body of the crime, or the substantial fact that a crime has been committed. Does any one doubt it in this case? It is true that no one actually saw the prisoner kill the decedent, and that he has so sucessfully hidden the body that it has not been found, but the powerful chain of circumstances, clear and close-linked, proving motive, the criminal agency, and the criminal act, is overwhelming.

"The victim in this case is on the eve of making a statement that would prove fatal to the prisoner. The night before the statement is to be made he goes to her residence. They quarrel. Her voice is heard, raised high in the greatest passion, denouncing him, and charging that he is a murderer, that she has the evidence and will reveal it, that he shall be hanged, and that he shall not be rid of her. Here is the motive for the crime, clear as light. Are not the bloody knife, the bloody dress, the bloody clothes of the prisoner, unimpeachable witnesses to the criminal act? The criminal agency of the prisoner has not the shadow of a possibility to obscure it. His motive is gigantic. The blood on him, and his despair when arrested, cry 'Murder! murder!' with a thousand tongues.

"Men may lie, but circumstances cannot. The thousand hopes and fears and passions of men may delude, or bias the witness. Yet it is beyond the human mind to conceive that a clear, complete chain of concatenated circumstances can be in error. Hence it is that the greatest jurists have declared that such evidence, being rarely liable to delusion or fraud, is safest and most powerful. The machinery of human justice cannot guard against the remote and improbable doubt. The inference is persistent in the affairs of men. It is the only means by which the human mind reaches the truth. If you forbid the jury to exercise it, you bid them work after first striking off their hands. Rule out the irresistible inference, and the end of justice is come in this land; and you may as well leave the spider to weave his web through the abandoned courtroom."

The attorney stopped, looked down at Mason with a pompous sneer, and retired to his place at the table. The judge sat thoughtful and motionless. The jurymen leaned forward in their seats.

"If your Honor please," said Mason, rising, "this is a matter of law, plain, clear, and so well settled in the State of New York that even counsel for the People should know it. The question before your Honor is simple. If the *corpus delicti,* the body of the crime, has been proven, as required by the laws of the commonwealth, then this case should go to the jury. If not, then it is the duty of this Court to direct the jury to find the prisoner not guilty. There is here no room for judicial discretion. Your Honor has but to recall and apply the rigid rule announced by our courts prescribing distinctly how the *corpus delicti* in murder must be proven.

"The prisoner here stands charged with the highest crime. The law demands, first, that the crime, as a fact, be established. The fact that the victim is indeed dead must first be made certain before any one can be convicted for her killing, because, so long as there remains the remotest doubt as to the death, there can be no certainty as to the criminal agent, although the circumstantial evidence indicating the guilt of the accused may be positive, complete, and utterly irresistible. In murder, the *corpus delicti*, or body of the crime, is composed of two elements:

"Death, as a result.

"The criminal agency of another as the means.

"It is the fixed and immutable law of this State, laid down in the leading case of Ruloff v. The People, and binding upon this Court, that both components of the *corpus delicti* shall not be established by circumstantial evidence. There must be direct proof of one or the other of these two component elements of the *corpus delicti*. If one is proven by direct evidence, the other may be presumed; but both shall not be presumed from circumstances, no matter how powerful, how cogent, or how completely overwhelming the circumstances may be. In other words, no man can be convicted of murder in the State of New York, unless the body of the victim be found and identified, or there be direct proof that the prisoner did some act adequate to produce death, and did it in such a manner as to account for the disappearance of the body."

The face of the judge cleared and grew hard. The members of the bar were attentive and alert; they were beginning to see the legal escape open up. The audience were puzzled; they did not yet understand. Mason turned to the counsel for the People. His ugly face was bitter with contempt.

"For three days," he said, "I have been tortured by this useless and expensive farce. If counsel for the People had been other than playactors, they would have known in the beginning that Victor Ancona could not be convicted for murder, unless he were confronted in this courtroom with a living witness, who had looked into the dead face of Nina San Croix; or, if not that, a living witness who had seen him drive the dagger into her bosom.

"I care not if the circumstantial evidence in this case were so strong and irresistible as to be overpowering; if the judge on the bench, if the jury, if every man within sound of my voice, were convinced of the guilt of the prisoner to the degree of certainty that is absolute; if the circumstantial evidence left in the mind no shadow of the remotest improbable doubt; yet, in the absence of the eye-witness, this prisoner cannot be punished, and this Court must compel the jury to acquit him." The audience now understood, and they were dumbfounded. Surely this was not the law. They had been taught that the law was common sense, and this,—this was anything else.

Mason saw it all, and grinned. "In its tenderness," he sneered, "the law shields the innocent. The good law of New York reaches out its hand and lifts the prisoner out of the clutches of the fierce jury that would hang him."

Mason sat down. The room was silent. The jurymen looked at each other in amazement. The counsel for the People arose. His face was white with anger, and incredulous.

"Your Honor," he said, "this doctrine is monstrous. Can it be said that, in order to evade punishment, the murderer has only to hide or destroy the body of the victim, or sink it into the sea? Then, if he is not seen to kill, the law is powerless and the murderer can snap his finger in the face of retributive justice. If this is the law, then the law for the highest crime is a dead letter. The great commonwealth winks at murder and invites every man to kill his enemy, provided he kill him in secret and hide him. I repeat, your Honor,"—the man's voice was now loud and angry and rang through the court-room—"that this doctrine is monstrous!"

"So said Best, and Story, and many another," muttered Mason, "and the law remained."

"The Court," said the judge, abruptly, "desires no further argument."

The counsel for the People resumed his seat. His face lighted up with triumph. The Court was going to sustain him.

The judge turned and looked down at the jury. He was grave, and spoke with deliberate emphasis.

"Gentlemen of the jury," he said, "the rule of Lord Hale obtains in this State and is binding upon me. It is the law as stated by counsel for the prisoner: that to warrant conviction of murder there must be direct proof either of the death, as of the finding and identification of the corpse, or of criminal violence adequate to produce death, and exerted in such a manner as to account for the disappearance of the body; and it is only when there is direct proof of the one that the other can be established by circumstantial evidence. This is the law, and cannot now be departed from. I do not presume to explain its wisdom. Chief-Justice Johnson has observed, in the leading case, that it may have its probable foundation in the idea that where direct proof is absent as to both the fact of the death and of criminal violence capable of producing death, no evidence can rise to the degree of moral certainty that the individual is dead by criminal intervention, or even lead by direct inference to this result; and that, where the fact of death is not certainly ascertained, all inculpatory circumstantial evidence wants the key necessary for its satisfactory interpretation, and cannot be depended on to furnish more than probable results. It may be, also, that such a rule has some reference to the dangerous possibility that a general preconception of guilt, or a general excitement of popular feeling, may creep in to supply the place of evidence, if, upon other than direct proof of death or a cause of death, a jury are permitted to pronounce a prisoner guilty.

"In this case the body has not been found and there is no direct proof of criminal agency on the part of the prisoner, although the chain of circumstantial evidence is complete and irresistible in the highest degree. Nevertheless, it is all circumstantial evidence, and under the laws of New York the prisoner cannot be punished. I have no right of discretion. The law does not permit a conviction in this case, although every one of us may be morally certain of the prisoner's guilt. I am, therefore, gentlemen of the jury, compelled to direct you to find the prisoner not guilty."

"Judge," interrupted the foreman, jumping up in the box, "we cannot find that verdict under our oath; we know that this man is guilty."

"Sir," said the judge, "this is a matter of law in which the wishes of the jury cannot be considered. The clerk will write a verdict of not guilty, which you, as foreman, will sign."

The spectators broke out into a threatening murmur that began to grow and gather volume. The judge rapped on his desk and ordered the bailiffs promptly to suppress any demonstration on the part of the audience. Then he directed the foreman to sign the verdict prepared by the clerk, When this was done he turned to Victor Ancona; his face was hard and there was a cold glitter in his eyes.

"Prisoner at the bar," he said, "you have been put to trial before this tribunal on a charge of cold-blooded and atrocious murder. The evidence produced against you was of such powerful and overwhelming character that it seems to have left no doubt in the minds of the jury, nor indeed in the mind of any person present in this court-room.

"Had the question of your guilt been submitted to these twelve arbiters, a conviction would certainly have resulted and the death penalty would have been imposed. But the law, rigid, passionless, even-eyed, has thrust in between you and the wrath of your fellows and saved you from it I do not cry out against the impotency of the law; it is perhaps as wise as imperfect humanity could make it. I deplore, rather, the genius of evil men who, by cunning design, are enabled to slip through the fingers of this law. I have no word of censure or admonition for you, Victor Ancona. The law of New York compels me to acquit you. I am only its mouthpiece, with my individual wishes throttled. I speak only those things which the law directs I shall speak.

"You are now at liberty to leave this court-room, not guiltless of the crime of murder, perhaps, but at least rid of its punishment. The eyes of men may see Cain's mark on your brow, but the eyes of the Law are blind to it."

When the audience fully realized what the judge had said they were amazed and silent. They knew as well as men could know, that Victor Ancona was guilty of murder, and yet he was now going out of the court-room free. Could it happen that the law protected only against the blundering rogue? They had heard always of the boasted completeness of the law which magistrates from time immemorial had labored to perfect, and now when the skilful villain sought to evade it, they saw how weak a thing it was.

V.

The wedding march of Lohengrin floated out from the Episcopal Church of St. Mark, clear and sweet, and perhaps heavy with its paradox of warning. The theatre of this coming contract before high heaven was a wilderness of roses worth the taxes of a county. The high caste of Manhattan, by the grace of the check-book, were present, clothed in Parisian purple and fine linen, cunningly and marvellously wrought.

Over in her private pew, ablaze with jewels, and decked with fabrics from the deft hand of many a weaver, sat Mrs. Miriam Steuvisant as imperious and self-complacent as a queen. To her it was all a kind of triumphal procession, proclaiming her ability as a general. With her were a choice few of the *genus homo* which obtains at the five-o'clock teas, instituted, say the sages, for the purpose of sprinkling the holy water of Lethe.

"Czarina," whispered Reggie Du Puyster, leaning forward, "I salute you. The ceremony *sub jugum* is superb."

"Walcott is an excellent fellow," answered Mrs. Steuvisant; "not a vice, you know, Reggie."

"Aye, Empress," put in the others, "a purist taken in the net. The clean-skirted one has come to the altar. Vive la vertu!"

Samuel Walcott, still sunburned from his cruise, stood before the chancel with the only daughter of the blue-blooded St. Clairs. His face was clear and honest and his voice firm. This was life and not romance. The lid of the sepulchre had closed and he had slipped from under it. And now, and ever after, the hand red with murder was clean as any.

The minister raised his voice, proclaiming the holy union before God, and this twain, half pure, half foul, now by divine ordinance one flesh, bowed down before it. No blood cried from the ground. The sunlight of high noon streamed down through the window panes like a benediction.

Back in the pew of Mrs. Miriam Steuvisant, Reggie Du Puyster turned down his thumb. "Habet!" he said.

II—TWO PLUNGERS OF MANHATTAN

I.

FOR my part, Sidney," said the dark man, "I don't agree with your faith in Providence at all. For the last ten years it has kept too far afield of our House in every matter of importance. It has never once shown its face to us except for the purpose of interposing some fatal wrecker just at the critical moment. Don't you remember how it helped Barton Woodlas rob our father in that shoe trust at Lynn? And you will recall the railroad venture of our own. Did not the cursed thing go into the hands of a receiver the very moment we had gotten the stock cornered? And look at the oil deal. Did not the tools stick in both test wells within fifty feet of the sand, and all the saints could not remove them? I tell you I have no faith in it. The same thing is going to happen again."

"There is some truth in your rant, brother," replied the light man, "but I cling to my superstition. We have a cool million in this thing, a cool million. If we can only break the Chicago corner the market is bound to turn. The thing is below the cost of production now, and this western combine is already groggy. Ten thousand would break its backbone, and leave us in a position to force the market up to the ceiling."

"But how in Heaven's name, Sidney, are we going to get the other five thousand? To-day at ten I put up everything that could be scraped together, begged, or borrowed, and out of it all we have scarcely five thousand dollars. For any good that amount will do we might as well have none at all. We know that this combine would in all probability weather a plunge of five thousand, while a bold plunge of ten thousand would rout it as certainly as there is a sun in heaven, but we only have half enough money and no means of getting another dollar. If there were ten millions in it the case would be the same. The jig is up."

"I don't think so, Gordon. I don't give it up. We must raise the money."

"Raise the money!" put in the other, bitterly; "as well talk of raising the soul of Samuel. Did n't I say that I had raised the last money that human ingenuity could raise; that there was not another shining thing left on earth to either of us, but our beauty?—And it would take genius to raise money on that, Sidney, gigantic genius."

He stopped, and looked at his brother. The brother poured his soda into the brandy, and said simply, "We must find it."

"You find it," said Gordon Montcure, getting up, and walking backward and forward across the room.

For full ten minutes Sidney Montcure studied the bottom of his glass. Then he looked up, and said, "Brother, do you remember the little bald-headed man who stopped us on the steps of the Stock Exchange last week?"

"Yes; you mean the old ghost with the thin, melancholy face?"

"The same. You remember he said that if we were ever in a desperate financial position we should come to the office building on the Wall Street corner and inquire for Randolph Mason, and that Mason would show us a way out of the difficulty; but that under no circumstances were we to say how we happened to come to him, except that we had heard of his ability."

"I recall the queer old chap well," said the other. "He seemed too clean and serious for a fakir, but I suppose that is what he was; unless he is wrong in the head, which is more probable."

"Do you know, brother," said Sidney Montcure, thrusting his hands into his pockets, "I have been thinking of him, and I have a great mind to go down there in the morning just for a flyer. If there is any such man as Randolph Mason, he is not a fakir, because I know the building, and he could not secure an office in any such prominent place unless he was substantial."

"That is true, although I am convinced that you will find Randolph

Mason a myth."

"At any rate, we have nothing to lose, brother; there may be something in it. Will you go with me to-morrow morning?"

The dark man nodded assent, and proceeded to add his autograph to the club's collection, as evidenced by its wine ticket.

Gordon and Sidney Montcure were high-caste club men of the New York type, brokers and plungers until three p.m., immaculate gentlemen thereafter. Both were shrewd men of the world. And as they left the Ephmere Club that night, that same club and divers shop-men of various guilds had heavy equitable interests in the success of their plans.

Shortly after ten the following morning, the two brothers entered the great building in which Randolph Mason was supposed to have his office. There, on the marble-slab directory, was indeed the name; but it bore no indication of his business, and simply informed the stranger that he was to be found on the second floor front. The two men stepped into the elevator, and asked the boy to show them to Mr. Mason's office. The boy put them off on the second floor, and directed them to enquire at the third door to the left. They found here a frosted glass door with "Randolph Mason, Counsellor," on an ancient silver strip fastened to the middle panel. Sidney Montcure opened the door, and the two entered. The office room into which they came was large and scrupulously clean.

The walls were literally covered with maps of every description. Two rows of mammoth closed bookcases extended across the room, and there were numerous file cases of the most improved pattern. At a big flat-topped table, literally heaped with letters, sat their friend, the little bald, melancholy man, writing as though his very life and soul were at stake.

"We desire to speak with Mr. Mason, sir," said Sidney Montcure, addressing the little man. The man arose, and went into the adjoining room. In a moment he returned and announced that Mr. Mason would see the gentlemen at once in his private office.

They found the private office of Randolph Mason to be in appearance much like the private office of a corporation attorney. The walls were lined with closed bookcases, and there were piles of plats and blue prints and bundles of papers scattered over a round-topped mahogany table.

Randolph Mason turned round in his chair as the men entered.

"Be seated, gentlemen," he said, removing his eye-glasses. "In what manner can I be of service?" His articulation was metallic and precise.

"We have had occasion to hear of your ability, Mr. Mason," said Gordon Montcure, "and we have called to lay our difficulty before you, in the hope that you may be able to suggest some remedy. It may be that our dilemma is beyond the scope of your vocation, as it is not a legal matter."

"Let me hear the difficulty," said Mason, bluntly.

"We are in a most unfortunate and critical position," said Gordon Montcure. "My brother and myself are members of the Board of Trade, and, in defiance of the usual rule, occasionally speculate for ourselves. After making elaborate and careful investigation, we concluded that the wheat market had reached bottom and was on the verge of a strong and unusual advance. We based this conclusion on two safe indications: the failure in production of the other staples, and the fact that the price of wheat was slightly below the bare cost of production. This status of the market we believed could not remain, and on Monday last we bought heavily on a slight margin. The market continued to fall. We covered our margins, and plunged, in order to bull the market. To our surprise the decline continued; we gathered all our ready money, and plunged again. The market wavered, but continued to decline slowly. Then it developed that there was a Chicago combine against us. We at once set about ascertaining the exact financial status of this combine, and discovered that it was now very weak, and that a bold plunge of ten thousand dollars would rout it. But unfortunately all our ready money was now gone. After exhausting every security and resorting to every imaginable means we have only five thousand dollars in all. This sum is utterly useless under the circumstances, for we know well that the combine would hold out against a plunge of this dimension and we would simply lose everything, while a bold, sudden plunge of ten thousand would certainly break the market and make us a vast fortune. Of course, no sane man will lend us money under circumstances of this kind, and it is not possible for us to raise another dollar on earth." The speaker leaned back in his chair, like a man who has stated what he knows to be a hopeless case. "We are consuming your time unnecessarily," he added; "our case is, of course, remediless."

Mason did not at once reply. He turned round in his chair and looked out of the open window. The two brothers observed him more closely. They noticed that his clothing was evidently of the best, that he was scrupulously neat and clean, and wore no ornament of any kind. Even the eyeglasses were attached to a black silk guard, and had a severely plain steel spring.

"Have you a middle name, sir?" he said, turning suddenly to Sidney Montcure.

"Yes," replied the man addressed, "Van Guilder; I am named for my grandfather."

"An old and wealthy family of this city, and well known in New England," said Mason; "that is fortunate." Then he bent forward and looking straight into the eyes of his clients said: "Gentlemen, if you are ready to do exactly what I direct, you will have five thousand dollars by to-morrow night. Is that enough?"

"Ample," replied Gordon Montcure; "and we are ready to follow your instructions to the letter in any matter that is not criminal."

"The transaction will be safely beyond the criminal statutes," said Mason, "although it is close to the border line of the law."

"'Beyond, is as good as a mile," said Gordon Montcure; "let us hear your plan."

"It is this," said Mason. "Down at Lynn, Massachusetts, there is a certain retired shoe manufacturer of vast wealth, accumulated by questionable transactions. He is now passing into the sixties, and, like every man of his position, is restless and unsatisfied. Five years ago he concluded to build a magnificent residence in the suburbs of Lynn. He spared nothing to make the place palatial in every respect. The work has been completed within the past summer. The grounds are superb, and the place is indeed princely. As long as the palace was in process of building, the old gentleman was interested and delighted; but no sooner was it finished than, like all men of his type, he was at once dissatisfied. He now thinks that he would like to travel on the continent, but he has constructed a Frankenstein Monster, which he imagines requires his personal care. He will not trust it to an agent, he does not dare to rent it, and he can find no purchaser for such a palace in such a little city. The mere fact that he cannot do exactly as he pleases is a source of huge vexation to such a man as old Barton Woodlas, of the Shoe Trust."

The two Montcures apparently gave no visible evidence of their mighty surprise and interest at the mention of the man who had robbed their father, yet Mason evidently saw something in the tail of their eyes, for he smiled with the lower half of his face, and continued: "You, sir," he said, speaking directly to Sidney Montcure, "must go to Lynn and buy this house in the morning."

"Buy the house!" answered the man, bitterly, "your irony approaches the sublime; we have only five thousand dollars and no security. How could we buy a house?"

"I am meeting the difficulties, if you please, sir," said Mason, "and not yourself. At ten tomorrow you must be at Lynn. At two p.m. you will call upon Barton Woodlas, giving your name as Sidney Van Guilder, from New York. He knows that family, and will at once presume your wealth. You will say to him that you desire to purchase a country place for your grandfather, and heard of his residence. The old gentleman will at once jump at this chance for a wealthy purchaser, and drive you out to his grounds. You will criticise somewhat and make some objections, but will finally conclude to purchase, if satisfactory terms can be made. Here you will find Barton Woodlas a shrewd business dealer, and you must follow my instructions to the very letter. He will finally agree to take about fifty thousand dollars. You will make the purchase proposing to pay down five thousand cash, and give a mortgage on the property for the residue of the purchase money, making short-time notes. Five thousand in hand and a mortgage will of course be safe, and the old gentleman will take it. You demand immediate possession, and as he is not residing in the house you will get it. Go with him at once to his attorney, pay the money, have the papers signed and recorded, and be in full possession of the property by four o'clock in the afternoon."

Mason stopped abruptly and turned to Gordon Montcure. "Sir," he said curtly, "I must ask you to step into the other office and remain until I have finished my instructions to your brother. I have found it best to explain to each individual that part of the transaction which he is expected to perform. Suggestions made in the presence of a third party invariably lead to disaster." Gordon Montcure went into the outer room and sat down. He was impressed by this strange interview with Mason. Here was certainly one of the most powerful and mysterious men he had ever met,—one whom he could not understand, who was a mighty enigma. But the man was so clear and positive that Montcure concluded to do exactly as he said. After all, the money they were risking was utterly worthless as matters now stood.

In a few moments Sidney Montcure came out of the private office and took a cab for the depot, leaving his brother in private interview with Randolph Mason.

II.

The following afternoon, Gordon Montcure stepped from the train at Lynn. An hour before, *en route*, he had received a telegram from Mason saying that the deal had been made and that his brother was in possession of the property, and authorizing him to proceed according to instructions. He was a man of business methods and began at once to play his part.

Calling a carriage, he went to the court-house and ascertained that the deed had been properly recorded. Then he drove to the hotel of Barton Woodlas and demanded to see that gentleman at once. He was shown into a private parlor and in a few minutes the shoe capitalist came down. He was a short, nervous, fat man with a pompous strut.

"Mr. Woodlas, I presume," said Gordon Mont-cure.

"The same, sir," was the answer; "to what am I indebted for this honor?"

"To be brief," replied Montcure, "I am looking for one Sidney Van Guilder. I am informed that he was to-day with you in this city. Can you tell me where I can see him?"

"Why, yes," said the old gentleman, anxiously; "I suppose he is out at the residence I to-day sold him for his grandfather. Is there anything wrong?"

"What?" cried Montcure, starting up, "You sold him a residence to-day? Curse the luck! I am too late. He is evidently into his old tricks."

"Old tricks," said the little fat man, growing pale, "what in Heaven's name is wrong with him? Speak out, man; speak out!"

"To come at once to the point," said Gordon Montcure, "Mr. Van Guilder is just a little offcolor. He is shrewd and all right in every way except for this one peculiarity. He seems to have an insane desire to purchase fine buildings and convert them into homes for his horses. He has attempted to change several houses on Fifth Avenue into palatial stables, and has only been prevented by the city authorities. In all human probability the house you have sold him will be full of stalls by morning."

"My house full of stalls!" yelled the little fat man, "my house that I have spent so much money on, and my beautiful grounds a barn-yard! Never! never! Come on, sir, come on, we must go there at once!" And Barton Woodlas waddled out of the room as fast as his short legs could carry him. Gordon Montcure followed, smiling.

Both men climbed into Montcure's carriage and hurried out to the suburban residence. The grounds were indeed magnificent, and the house a palace. As they drove in, they noticed several Italian laborers digging a trench across the lawn. Barton Woodlas tumbled out of the carriage and bolted into the house, followed by Montcure. Here they found a scene of the greatest confusion. The house was filled with grimy workmen. They were taking off the doors and shutters, and removing the stairway, and hammering in different portions of the house until the noise was like bedlam.

Sidney Van Guilder stood in the drawing-room, with his coat off, directing his workmen. His clothing was disarranged and dusty but he was apparently enthusiastic and happy. "Stop, sir! stop!" cried Barton Woodlas, waving his arms and rushing into the room. "Put these dirty workmen out of here and stop this vandalism at once! At once!"

Sidney Van Guilder turned round smiling. "Ah," he said, "is it you, Mr. Woodlas? I am getting on swimmingly you see. This will make a magnificent stable. I can put my horses on both floors, but I will be compelled to cut the inside all out, and make great changes. It is a pity that you built your rooms so big."

For a moment the little man was speechless with rage; then he danced up and down and yelled: "Oh, you crazy fool! You crazy fool! You are destroying my house! It won't be worth a dollar!"

"I beg your pardon," said Van Guilder, coldly, "this is my house and I shall do with it as I like. I have bought it and I shall make a home for my horses of it by morning. It cannot possibly be any business of yours."

"No business of mine!" shouted Woodlas, "what security have I but the mortgage? And if you go on with this cursed gutting the mortgage won't be worth a dollar. Oh, my beautiful house! My beautiful house! It is awful, awful! Come on, sir," he yelled to Gordon Montcure, "I will find a way to stop the blooming idiot!"

With that he rushed out of the house and rolled into the carriage, Gordon Montcure following. Together the two men were driven furiously to the office of Vinson Harcout, counsellor for the Shoe Trust.

That usually placid and unexcitable gentleman turned round in astonishment as the two men bolted into his private office. Woodlas dropped into a chair and, between curses and puffs of exhaustion, began to describe his trouble. When the lawyer had finally succeeded in drawing from the irate old man a full understanding of the matter, he leaned back in his chair and stroked his chin thoughtfully.

"Well," he said, "this is an unfortunate state of affairs, but there is really no legal remedy for it. The title to the property is in Mr. Van Guilder. He is in possession by due and proper process of law, and he can do as he pleases, even to the extent of destroying the property utterly. If he chooses to convert his residence into a stable, he certainly commits no crime and simply exercises a right which is legally his own. It is true that you have such equitable interest in the property that you might be able to stop him by injunction proceedings—we will try that at any rate."

The attorney stopped and turned to his stenographer. "William," he said, "ask the clerk if Judge Henderson is in the court-room." The young man went to the telephone and returned in a moment. "Judge Henderson is not in the city, sir," he said. "The clerk answers that he went to Boston early in the day to meet with some judicial committee from New York and will not return until to-morrow."

The lawyer's face lengthened. "Well," he said, "that is the end of it. We could not possibly reach him in time to prevent Mr. Van Guilder from carrying out his intentions."

Gordon Montcure smiled grimly. Mason had promised to inveigle away the resident judge by means of a bogus telegram, and he had done so.

"Oh!" wailed the little fat man, "is there no law to keep me from being ruined? Can't I have him arrested, sir?"

"Unfortunately, no," replied the lawyer. "He is committing no crime, he is simply doing what he has a full legal right to do if he so chooses, and neither you nor any other man can interfere with him. If you attempt it, you at once become a violator of the law and proceed at your peril. You are the victim of a grave wrong, Mr. Woodlas. Your security is being destroyed and great loss may possibly result. Yet there is absolutely no remedy except the possible injunction, which, in the absence of the judge, is no remedy at all. It is an exasperating and unfortunate position for you, but, as I said, there is nothing to be done."

The face of Barton Woodlas grew white and his jaw dropped. "Gone!" he muttered, "all gone, five thousand dollars and a stable as security for forty thousand! It is ruin, ruin!"

"I am indeed sorry," said the cold-blooded attorney, with a feeling of pity that was unusual, "but there is no remedy, unless perhaps you could repurchase the property before it is injured."

"Ah," said the little fat man, straightening up in his chair, "I had not thought of that. I will do it. Come on, both of you," and he hurried to the carriage without waiting for an answer.

At the residence in question the three men found matters as Barton Woodlas had last seen them, except that the trench across the lawn was now half completed and the doors and shutters had all been removed from the house and piled up on the veranda.

Sidney Van Guilder laughed at their proposition to repurchase. He assured them that he had long been looking for just this kind of property, that it suited him perfectly, and that he would not think of parting with it. The attorney for Wood-las offered two thousand dollars' advance; then three, then four, but Sidney Van Guilder was immovable. Finally Gordon Montcure suggested that perhaps the city would not allow his stable to remain after he had completed it, and advised him to name some price for the property. Van Guilder seemed to consider this possibility with some seriousness. He had presumably had this trouble in New York City, and finally said that he would take ten thousand dollars for his bargain. Old Barton Woodlas fumed and cursed and ground his teeth, and damned every citizen of the State of New York from the coast to the lakes for a thief, a villain, and a robber.

Finally, when the Italians began to cut through the wall of the drawing-room and the fat old gentleman's grief and rage were fast approaching apoplexy, the lawyer raised his offer to seven thousand dollars cash, and Sidney Van Guilder reluctantly accepted it and dismissed his workmen. The four went at once to the law office of Vinson Harcout, where the mortgage and notes were cancelled, the money paid, and the deed prepared, reconveying the property and giving Barton Woodlas immediate possession.

III.

At nine-thirty the following morning, the two brothers walked into the private office of Randolph Mason and laid down seven thousand dollars on his desk. Mason counted out two thousand and thrust it into his pocket. "Gentlemen," he said shortly, "here is the five thousand dollars which I promised. I commend you for following my instructions strictly."

"We have obeyed you to the very letter," said Gordon Montcure, handing the money to his brother, "except in one particular."

"What!" cried Mason, turning upon him, "you dared to change my plans?"

"No," said Gordon Montcure, stepping back, "only the fool lawyer suggested the repurchase before I could do it."

"Ah," said Randolph Mason, sinking back into his chair, "a trifling detail. I bid you goodmorning."

III—WOODFORD'S PARTNER

[See Clark's Criminal Law, p. 274, or any good text-book for the general principles of law herein concerned. See especially State vs. Reddick, 48 Northwestern Reporter, 846, and the long list of cases there cited, on the proposition that the taking of partnership funds by one of the general partners, even with felonious intent, constitutes no crime. Also, Gary vs. Northwestern Masonic Aid Association, 53 Northwestern Reporter, 1086.]

I.

AFTER some thirty years, one begins to appreciate in a slight degree the mystery of things in counter-distinction to the mystery of men. He learns with dumb horror that startling and unforeseen events break into the shrewdest plans and dash them to pieces utterly, or with grim malice wrench them into engines of destruction, as though some mighty hand reached out from the darkness and shattered the sculptor's marble, or caught the chisel in his fingers and drove it back into his heart.

As one grows older, he seeks to avoid, as far as may be, the effect of these unforeseen interpositions, by carrying in his plans a factor of safety, and, as what he is pleased to call his "worldly wisdom" grows, he increases this factor until it is a large constant running through all his equations dealing with probabilities of the future. Whether in the end it has availed anything, is still, after six thousand years, a mooted question. Nevertheless, it is the manner of men to calculate closely in their youth, disregarding the factor of safety, and ignoring utterly the element of Chance, Fortune, ar Providence, as it may please men to name this infinite meddling intelligence. Whether this arises from ignorance or some natural unconscious conviction that it is useless to strive against it, the race has so far been unable to determine. That it is useless to, the weight of authorities would seem to indicate, while, on the other hand, the fact that men are amazed and dumbfounded when they first realize the gigantic part played by this mysterious power in all human affairs, and immediately thereafter plan to evade it, would tend to the conviction that there might be some means by which these startling accidents could be guarded against, or at least their effect counteracted.

The laws, if in truth there be any, by which these so-called fortunes and misfortunes come to men, are as yet undetermined, except that they arise from the quarter of the unexpected, and by means oftentimes of the commonplace.

On a certain Friday evening in July, Carper Harris, confidential clerk of the great wholesale house of Beaumont, Milton, & Company of Baltimore, was suddenly prostrated under the horror of this great truth. For the first time in his life Fate had turned about and struck him, and the blow had been delivered with all her strength.

Up to this time he had been an exceedingly fortunate man. To begin with, he had been born of a good family, although, at the time of his father's death, reduced in circumstances. While quite a small boy, he had been taken in as clerk through the influence of Mr. Milton, who had been a friend of his father. The good blood in the young man had told from the start. He had shown himself capable and unusually shrewd in business matters, and had risen rapidly to the position of chief confidential clerk. In this position he was intrusted with the most important matters of the firm, and was familiar with all its business relations. His abilities had expanded with the increasing duties of his successive positions. He had done the firm much service, and had shown himself to be a most valuable and trustworthy man. But, with it all, the eyes of old Silas Beaumont had followed his every act, in season and out of season, tirelessly. It was a favorite theory of old Beaumont, that the great knave was usually the man of irreproachable habits, and necessarily the man of powerful and unusual abilities, and that, instead of resorting to ordinary vices or slight acts of rascality, he was wont to bide his time until his reputation gained him opportunity for some gigantic act of dishonesty, whereby he could make a vast sum at one stroke.

Old Beaumont was accustomed to cite two scriptural passages as the basis of his theory, one being that oft-quoted remark of David in his haste, and the other explanatory of what the Lord saw when he repented that he had made man on the earth.

Like all those of his type, when this theory had once become fixed with him, he sought on all occasions for instances by which to demonstrate its truthfulness. Thus it happened that the honesty and industry of young Harris were the very grounds upon which Beaumont based his suspicions and his acts of vigilance.

When it was proposed that Carper Harris should go to Europe in order to buy certain grades of pottery which the firm imported, Beaumont grumbled and intimated that it was taking a large risk to intrust money to him. He said the sum was greater than the young man had been accustomed to handle, that big amounts of cash were dangerous baits, and then he switched over to his theory and hinted that just this kind of opportunity would be the one which a man would seize for his master act of dishonesty. The other members of the firm ridiculed the idea, and arranged the matter over Silas Beaumont's protest.

Thus it happened that about seven o'clock on the eventful Friday, Carper Harris left Baltimore for New York. He carried a small hand-bag containing twenty thousand dollars, with which he was to buy foreign exchange. Arriving at the depot he had checked his luggage and had gone into the chair-car with only his overcoat and the little hand-bag. He laid his overcoat across the back of the seat and set the little satchel down in the seat beside him. He had been particularly careful that the money should be constantly guarded, and for that reason he had attempted to keep his hand on the handle of the bag during the entire trip, although he was convinced that there was no danger or risk of any consequence, for the reason that no one would suspect that the satchel contained cash. When he arrived in New York he had gone directly to his hotel and asked to be shown up to his room. It was his intention to look over the money carefully and see that it was all right, after which he would have it placed in one of the deposit boxes in the hotel safe until morning.

When Harris set the hand-bag down on the table under the light, after the servant had left the room, something about its general appearance struck his attention, and he bent down to examine it closely. As he did so his heart seemed to leap into his throat, and the cold perspiration burst out on his forehead and began to run down his face in streams. The satchel before him on the table was not the one in which he had placed the money in Baltimore, and with which he had left the counting-house of Beaumont, Milton, & Company. The young man attempted to insert the key in the lock of the satchel, but his hand trembled so that he could not do it, and in an agony of fear he threw down the keys and wrenched the satchel open. His great fear was only too well founded. The satchel contained a roll of newspapers. For a moment Carper Harris stood dazed and dumbfounded by his awful discovery; then he sank down in a heap on the floor and covered his face with his hands.

Of all the dreaded calamities that Fate could have sent, this was the worst. All that he had hoped for and labored for was gone by a stroke,— wiped out ruthlessly, and by no act or wrong of his. The man sat on the floor like a child, and literally wrung his hands in anguish, and strove to realize all the terrible results that would follow in the wake of this unforeseen calamity.

First of all there was Beaumont's theory, and the horror of the thought gripped his heart like a frozen hand. It stood like some grim demon barring the only truthful and honorable way out of the matter. How could he go back and say that he had been robbed. Beaumont would laugh the idea to scorn and gloat over the confirmation of his protest. Little would explanation avail. His friends would turn against him, and join with Beaumont, and seek to make the severity of their accusation against him atone for their previous trust and confidence, and their disregard of what they would now characterize as Mr. Beaumont's unusual foresight. And then, if they would listen to explanation, what explanation was there to make? He had left their counting-house with the money in the afternoon, and now in New York in the evening he claimed to have been robbed.

And how? That some one had substituted another hand-bag for the one with which he started, without attacking him and even without his slightest suspicion—a probable story indeed! Why, the hand-bag there on the table was almost exactly like the one he had taken with him to the company's office. No one but himself could tell that it was not the same bag. The whole matter would be considered a shrewd trick on his part,— a cunningly arranged scheme to rob his employers of this large sum of money. In his heated fancy he could see the whole future as it would come. The hard smile of incredulity with which his story would be greeted,—the arrest that would follow,—the sensational newspaper reports of the defalcation of Carper Harris, confidential clerk of the great wholesale house of Beaumont, Milton, & Company. The newspapers would assume his guilt, as they always do when one is charged with crime; they would speak of him as a defaulter, and would comment on the story as an ingenious defence emanating from his shrewd counsel. Even the newsboys on the street would convict him with the cry of, "All about the trial of the great defaulter!" The jury its very self, when it went into the box, would be going there to try a man already convicted of crime. This conviction would have been forced upon them by the reports, and they could not entirely escape from it, no matter how hard they might try. Why, if one of them should be asked suddenly what he was doing, in all possibility, if he should reply without stopping to think, he would answer that he was trying the man who had robbed Beaumont, Milton, & Company. So that way was barred, and it was a demon with a flaming sword that kept it.

The man arose and began to pace the floor. He could not go back and tell the truth. What other thing could he do? It was useless to inform the police. That would simply precipitate the storm. It would be going by another path the same way which he had convinced himself was so effectually blocked. Nor did he dare to remain silent. The loss would soon be discovered, and then his silence would convict him, while flight was open confession of the crime.

Carper Harris had one brother living in New York,—a sort of black sheep of the family, who had left home when a child to hazard his fortunes with the cattle exporters. The family had attempted to control him, but without avail. He had shifted around the stock-yards in Baltimore, and had gone finally to New York, and was now a commission merchant, with an office in Jersey City. The relation between this man and the family had been somewhat strained, but now, in the face of this dreaded disaster, Harris felt that he was the only one to appeal to—not that he hoped that his brother could render him any assistance, but because he must consult with some one, and this man was after all the only human being whom he could trust.

He hastily scribbled a note, and, calling a messenger, sent it to his brother's hotel. Then he threw himself down on the bed and covered his face with his hands. What diabolical patience and cunning Fate sometimes exhibits! All the good fortune which had come to young Harris seemed to have been only for the purpose of smoothing the way into this trap.

II.

What is wrong here, Carper?" said William Harris, as he shut the door behind him. "I expected to find a corpse from the tone of your note. What's up?"

The commission merchant was a short heavy young man with a big square jaw and keen gray eyes. His face indicated bull-dog tenacity and unlimited courage of the sterner sort.

Carper Harris arose when his brother entered. He was as white as the dead. "William," he said, "I wish I were a corpse!"

"Ho! ho!" cried the cattle-man, dropping into a chair. "There is a big smash-up on the track, that is evident. Which is gone, your girl or your job?"

"Brother," continued Carper Harris, "I am in a more horrible position than you can imagine. I don't know whether you will believe me or not, but if you don't, no one will."

"You may be a fool, Carper," answered the commission merchant, closing his hands, on the arms of his chair, "but you are not a liar. Go on, tell me the whole thing."

Carper Harris drew up a chair to the table and began to go over the whole affair from the beginning to the end. As he proceeded, the muscles of his brother's face grew more and more rigid, until they looked as hard and as firm as a cast. When he finally finished and dropped back into his chair, the cattle-man arose and without a word went over to the window, and stood looking out over the city, with his hands behind his back. There was no indication by which one could have known of the bitter struggle going on in the man's bosom, unless one could have looked deep into his eyes; there the danger and despair which he realized as attendant upon this matter shone through in a kind of fierce glare.

Finally he turned round and looked down half smilingly at his brother. "Well, Carper," he said, "is that all the trouble? We can fix that all right."

"How?" almost screamed young Harris, bounding to his feet, "how?"

The commission merchant came back leisurely to his chair and sat down. His features were composed and wore an air of pleasant assurance. "My boy," he began, "this is tough lines, to be sure, but you are worth a car-load of convicts yet. Sit down then, and I will straighten this thing out in a jiffy. I have been devilish lucky this season, and I now have about sixteen thousand dollars in bank. You have, I happen to know, some five thousand dollars in securities which came to you out of father's estate when it was settled. Turn these securities over to me and go right on to Europe as you intended. I will realize on the securities, and with the money I now have will be enabled to purchase the exchange which you require, and will have it sent to you immediately, so there will be no delay. You can go right on with your business as you intended, and neither old Beaumont nor any other living skinflint will ever know of this robbery."

Carper Harris could not speak. His emotion choked him. He seized his brother's hand and wrung it in silence, while the tears streamed down his face.

"Come, come," said the cattle-man, "this won't do! Brace up! I am simply lending you the money. You can return it if you ever get able. If you don't, why, it came easy, and I won't ever miss the loss of it."

"May God bless you, brother!" stammered Carper Harris. "You have saved me from the very grave, and what is more—from the stigma of a felon. You shall not lose this money by me. I will repay it if Heaven spares my life."

"Don't go on like a play-actor, Carper," said the cattle-man, rising and turning to the door. "Pull yourself together, gather up your duds, and skip out to London. The stuff will be there by the time you are ready for it." Then he went out and closed the door behind him.

<hr>

III.

Ihad to lie to him," said William Harris. "There was no other way out of it. I knew it was the only means by which I could get him out of the country. If he stayed here they would nab him and put him in the penitentiary in spite of the very devil himself. It is all very well to talk about even-eyed justice and all that rot, but a young man in that kind of a position would have about as much show as a snowball in Vesuvius. The best thing to do was to put him over the pond, and the next thing was to come here. I did both, now what is to be done?"

"It is evident," said Randolph Mason, "that the young man is the victim of one of our numerous gangs of train robbers, and it is quite as evident that it is utterly impossible to recover the stolen money. The thing to be done is to shift the loss."

"Shift the loss, sir," echoed the cattle-man; "I don't believe that I quite catch your meaning."

"Sir," said Mason, "the law of self-preservation is the great law governing the actions of men. All other considerations are of a secondary nature. The selfish interest is the great motive power. It is the natural instinct to seek vicarious atonement. Men do not bear a hurt if the hurt can be placed upon another. It is a bitter law, but it is, nevertheless, a law as fixed as gravity."

"I see," said the commission merchant; "but how is this loss to be shifted on any one? The money is gone for good; there is no way to get it back, and there is no means by which we can switch the responsibility to the shoulders of any other person. The money was placed in Carper Harris's custody, he was instructed to use great care in order to prevent any possible loss. He left Baltimore with it. The story of his robbery would only render him ridiculous if it were urged in his behalf. He alone is responsible for the money; there is no way to shift it."

"I said, sir," growled Mason, "that the loss must be shifted. What does the responsibility matter, provided the burden of loss can be placed upon other shoulders? How much money have you?"

"Only the five thousand dollars which I received from the sale of his securities," answered the man. "The story which I told him about the sixteen thousand was all a lie; I have scarcely a thousand dollars to my name, all told."

Mason looked at the cattle-man and smiled grimly. "So far you have done well," he said; "it seems that you must be the instrument through which this cunning game of Fate is to be blocked. You are the strong one; therefore the burden must fall on your shoulders. Are you ready to bear the brunt of this battle?"

"I am," said the man, quietly; "the boy must be saved if I have to go to Sing Sing for the next twenty years."

IV.

The traveller crossing the continent in a Pullman car is convinced that West Virginia is one continuous mountain. He has no desire to do other than to hurry past with all the rapidity of which the iron horse is capable. He can have no idea that in its central portion is a stretch of rolling blue-grass country, as fertile and as valuable as the stock-farm lands of Kentucky; with a civilization, too, distinctly its own, and not to be met with in any other country of the world. It seems to combine, queerly enough, certain of the elements of the Virginia planter, the western ranchman, and the feudal baron. Perhaps nowhere in any of the United States can be found such decided traces of the ancient feudal system as in this inland basin of West Virginia, surrounded by great mountain ranges, and for many generations cut off from active relations with the outside world. Nor is this civilization of any other than natural growth. In the beginning, those who came to this region were colonial families of degree,—many of them Tories, hating Washington and his government, and staunch lovers of the king at heart, for whom the more closely settled east and south were too unpleasant after the success of the Revolution. Many of them found in this fertile land lying against the foot-hills, and difficult of access from either the east or west, the seclusion and the utter absence of relations with their fellows which they so much desired. With them they brought certain feudal customs as a basis for the civilization which they builded. The nature of the country forced upon them others, and the desire for gain—ever large in the Anglo-Saxon heart—brought in still other customs, foreign and incongruous.

Thus it happened that at an early day this country was divided into great tracts, containing thousands of acres of grass lands, owned by certain powerful families, who resided upon it, and, to a very large extent, preserved ancient customs and ancient ideas in relation to men. The idea of a centrally situated manor-house was one adhered to from the very first, and this differed from the Virginia manor in that it was more massive and seemed to be built with the desire of strength predominating, as though the builder had yet in mind a vague notion of baronial defences, and some half hope or half fear of grim fights, in which he and his henchmen would defend against the invader. Gradually, after the feudal custom, the owner of one of these great tracts gathered about him a colony of tenants and retainers, who looked after his stock and grew to be almost fixtures of the realty and partook in no degree of the shiftless qualities of the modern tenant. They were attached to the family of the master of the estate, and shared in his peculiarities and his prejudices. His quarrel became their own, and personal conflicts between the retainers of different landowners were not infrequent. At such times, if the breaches of the peace were of such a violent order as to attract the attention of the law, the master was in honor bound to shield his men as far as possible, and usually his influence was sufficient to preserve them from punishment.

Indeed it was the landowner and his people against the world. They were different from the Virginians in that they were more aggressive and powerful, and were of a more adventurous and hardy nature. They were never content to be mere farmers, or to depend upon the cultivation of the soil. Nor were they careful enough to become breeders of fine stock. For these reasons it came about that they adopted a certain kind of stock business, combining the qualities of the ranch and the farm. They bought in the autumn great herds of two-year-old cattle, picking them up along the borders of Virginia and Kentucky. These cattle they brought over the mountains in the fall, fed them through the winter, and turned them out in the spring to fatten on their great tracts of pasture land. In the summer this stock was shipped to the eastern market and sold in favorable competition with the corn-fed stock of the west, and the stable-fed cattle of Virginia and Pennsylvania. As this business grew, the little farmer along the border began to breed the finer grades of stock. This the great landowners encouraged, and as the breeds grew better, the stock put upon the market from this region became more valuable, until at length the blue-grass region of West Virginia has become famous for its beef cattle, and for many years its cattle have been almost entirely purchased by the exporters for the Liverpool market.

So famous have the cattle of certain of these great landowners become, that each season the exporters send men to buy the stock, and not infrequently contract for it from year to year. Often a landowner, in whom the speculative spirit is rife, will buy up the cattle and make great contracts with the exporter, or he will form a partnership with an eastern commission merchant and ship with the market. The risks taken in this business are great, and often vast sums of money are made or lost in a week. It is a hazardous kind of gambling for the reason that great amounts are involved, and the slightest fall in the market will often result in big loss. With the shipping feature of this business have grown certain customs. Sometimes partnerships will be formed to continue for one or more weeks, and for the purpose of shipping. One drove of cattle or a number of droves; and when the shippers are well known the cattle are not paid for until the shipper returns from the market, it being presumed that he would not carry in bank sufficient money to pay for a large drove.

It is a business containing all the peril and excitement of the stock exchange, and all its fascinating hope of gain, as well as its dreaded possibility of utter ruin. Often in a grimy caboose at the end of a slow freight train is as true and fearless a devotee of Fortune, and as reckless a plunger as one would find in the pit on Wall Street, and not infrequently one with as vast plans and as heavy a stake in the play as his brother of the city. Yet to look at him—big, muscular, and uncouth—one would scarcely suspect that every week he was juggling with values ranging from ten to sixty thousand dollars.

One Monday morning of July, William Harris, a passenger on the through St. Louis express of the Baltimore & Ohio, said to the conductor that he desired to get off at Bridgeport, a small shipping station in this blue-grass region of West Virginia. The conductor answered that his train did not stop at this station, but that as the town was on a grade at the mouth of a tunnel he would slow up sufficiently for Mr. Harris to jump off if he desired to assume the risk. This Harris concluded to do, and accordingly, as the train ran by the long open platform beside the cattle pens, he swung himself down from the steps of the car and jumped. The platform was wet, and as Harris struck the planks his feet slipped and he would have fallen forward directly under the wheels of the coach had it not been that a big man standing near by sprang forward and dragged him back.

"You had a damned close call there, my friend," said the big man.

"Yes," said Harris, picking himself up, "you cut the undertaker out of a slight fee by your quick work."

The stranger turned sharply when he heard Harris's voice and grasped him by the hand. "Why, Billy," he said, "I did n't know it was you. What are you doing out here?"

"Well, well!" said Harris, shaking the man's hand vigorously, "there is a God in Israel sure. You are the very man I am looking for, Woodford."

Thomas Woodford was a powerfully built man—big, and muscular as an ox. He was about forty, a man of property, and a cattle-shipper known through the whole country as a daring speculator of almost phenomenal success. His plans were often gigantic, and his very rashness seemed to be the means by which good fortune heaped its favors upon him. He was in good humor this morning. The reports from the foreign markets were favorable, and indications seemed to insure the probability of a decidedly substantial advance at home. He put his big hand upon Harris's arm and fairly led him down the platform. "What is up, Billy?" he asked, lowering his voice.

"In my opinion," answered Harris, "the big combine among the exporters is going to burst and go up higher than Gilderoy's kite, and if we can get over to New York in time, we will have the world by the tail."

"Holy-head-of-the-church!" exclaimed the cattle-shipper, dropping his hands. "It will be every man for himself, and they will have to pay whatever we ask. But we must get over there this week. Next week everything that wears hoofs will be dumped into Jersey City. Come over to the hotel and let us hold a council of war."

The two men crossed the railroad track and entered the little eating-house which bore the high-sounding and euphonious title of "Hotel Holloway." They went directly up the steps and into a small room in the front of the building overlooking the railroad. Here Woodford locked the door, pulled off his coat, and took a large chew of tobacco. It was his way of preparing to wrestle with an emergency—a kind of mechanical means of forcing his faculties to a focus.

"Now, Billy," he said, "how is the best way to begin?"

Harris drew up his chair beside the bed on which his companion had seated himself.

"The situation is in this kind of shape," he began.

"The exporters have all the ships chartered and expect Ball & Holstein to furnish the cattle for next week's shipments. I believe that old Ball will kick out of the combine and tell the other exporters in the trust that they may go to the devil for their cattle. You know what kind of a panic this will cause. The space on the boats has been chartered and paid for, and it would be a great loss to let it stand empty. Nor could they ship the common stock on the market. All these men have foreign contracts, made in advance and calling for certain heavy grades of stock, and they are under contract to furnish a certain specified number of bullocks each week. They formed the combine in order to avoid difficulties, and have depended on a pool of all the stock contracted for by the several firms, out of which they could fill their boats when the supply should happen to be short or the market temporarily high. The foreign market is rising, and the old man is dead sure to hold on to the good thing in his clutches. I was so firmly convinced that the combine was going to pieces that I at once jumped on the first train west and hurried here to see you. The exporters must fill their contracts no matter what happens. If old Ball kicks over, as he is sure to do, the market will sail against the sky. We will have them on the hip if we can get the export cattle into New York, but we have no time to lose. These cattle must be bought to-day, and carred here to-morrow. Do you understand me?"

"Yes," said the cattle-shipper, striking his clenched right hand into the palm of his left. "It is going to be quick work, but we can do it or my name is not Woodford."

"We must have at least twelve carloads of big export cattle," continued Harris. "Not one to weigh less than sixteen hundred pounds. They must be good. Now, where can you get them quickest?"

"Well," answered the shipper, thoughtfully, "old Ralph Izzard has the best drove, but he wants five cents for them, and that is steep, too steep."

"No," said Harris, "that is all right if they are good. We have no time to run over the country to hunt them up. If these are the right kind we will not stand on his price."

"You can stake your soul on them being the right kind, Billy," answered the cattle-shipper enthusiastically. "Izzard picked them out of a drove of at least a thousand last fall, and he has looked after the brutes and pampered them like pet cats. They will go over sixteen hundred, every one of them, and they are as fat as hogs and as broad on the backs as a bed. I could slip out to his place and buy them to-night and have them here in time to car to-morrow, if you think we can give the old man his price."

"They will bring six and a half in New York, and go like hot cakes," said Harris, "but you will have to get out of this quick or you may run into a crowd of buyers from Baltimore."

"All right, Billy," said the cattle-shipper, rising and pulling on his coat, "I will tackle the old man to-night. We had better go to Clarksburg, and there you can lay low, and can come up to-morrow on the freight that stops here for the cattle. I will go out to Izzard's from there, and drive here by noon to-morrow. The accommodation will be along in about a half hour. I will go down and order the cars."

"Wait a moment, Woodford," said Harris, "we ought to have some written agreement about this business."

"What is the use?" answered the shipper. "We will go in even on it, but if you want to fix up a little contract, go ahead, and I will sign it. By the way, old Izzard is a little closer than most anybody else; we may have to pay him something down."

"I thought about that," said Harris, "and I brought some money with me, but I did n't have time to gather up much. I have about six thousand dollars here. Can you piece out with that?"

"Easy," replied the shipper. "The old devil would not have the nerve to ask more than ten thousand down."

William Harris seated himself at the table and drew up a memorandum of agreement between them, stating that they had formed a partnership for the purpose of dealing in stock, and had put into it ten thousand dollars as a partnership fund; that they were to share the profits or losses equally between them, and that the partnership was to continue for thirty days. This agreement both men signed, and Harris placed it in his pocket. Then the two men ordered the cattle cars for the following day and went to Clarksburg on the evening train.

Here Harris asked Woodford if he should pay over to him the five thousand dollars or put it in the bank. To this the cattle-shipper replied that he did not like to take the risk of carrying money over the country, and that it would be best to deposit it and check it out as it should be needed.

Woodford and Harris went to the bank. The shipper drew five thousand dollars from his own private account, put it with the five thousand which Harris handed him, and thrust the package of bills through the window to the teller.

"How do you wish to deposit this money, gentlemen?" asked the officer.

"I don't know, hardly," said the shipper, turning to his companion; "what do you think about it, Billy?"

"Well," said the commission-merchant, thoughtfully, "I suppose we had better deposit it in the firm name of Woodford & Harris, then you can give your checks that way and they wont get mixed with your private matters."

"That is right," said the cattle-shipper, "put it under the firm name." Whereupon the teller deposited the money subject to the check of Woodford & Harris.

"Now, Billy," continued Woodford, as they passed out into the street, "I will buy these cattle and put them on the train to-morrow. You go down with them. I will stay here and look over the country for another drove, and, if you want more, telegraph me."

"That suits me perfectly," replied Harris. "I must get back to New York, and I can wire you just how matters stand the moment I see the market." Then the two men shook hands and Harris returned to his hotel.

The following afternoon William Harris went to Bridgeport on the freight train. There he found twelve cars loaded with cattle, marked "Woodford & Harris." At Grafton he hired a man to go through with the stock, and took the midnight express for New York.

The partnership formed to take advantage of the situation which Harris had so fluently described, had been brought about with ease and expedition. Woodford was well known to William Harris. He had met him first in Baltimore where young Harris was a mere underling of one of the great exporting firms. Afterwards he had seen him frequently in Jersey City, and of late had sold some stock for him. The whole transaction was in close keeping with the customs of men in this business.

The confidence of one average cattle-man in another is a matter of more than passing wonder. Yet almost from time immemorial it has been respected, and instances are rare indeed where this confidence has been betrayed to any degree. Perhaps after all the ancient theory that "trust reposed breeds honesty in men," has in it a large measure of truthfulness, and if practised universally might result in huge elevation of the race. And it may be, indeed, that those who attempt to apply this principle to the business affairs of men are philanthropists of no little stature. But it is at best a dangerous experiment, wherein the safeguards of society are lowered, and whereby grievous wrongs break in and despoil the citizen.

To the view of one standing out from the circle of things, men often present queer contradictions. They call upon the state to protect them from the petty rogue and make no effort to protect themselves from the great one. They place themselves voluntarily in positions of peril, and then cry out bitterly if by any mishap they suffer hurt from it, and fume and rail at the law, when it is themselves they should rail at. The wonder is that the average business man is not ruined by the rogue. Surely the ignorance of the knave will not protect him always.

The situation would seem to arise from a false belief that the protection of the law is a great shield, covering at all points against the attacks of wrong.

V.

On Saturday afternoon about three o'clock, the cashier of the Fourth National Bank in the town of Clarksburg called Thomas Woodford as he was passing on the street, and requested him to come at once into the directors' room. Woodford saw by the man's face that there was something serious the matter and he hurried after him to the door of the private office. As he entered, Mr. Izzard arose and crossed the room to him. The old man held a check in his hand and was evidently laboring under great excitement.

"Woodford," he cried, thrusting the check up into the cattle-shipper's face, "this thing is not worth a damn! There is no money here to pay it."

"No money to pay it!" echoed Woodford. "You must be crazy. We put the money in here Monday. There's ten thousand dollars here to pay it."

"Well," said the old man, trembling with anger, "there is none here now. You gave me this check Tuesday on my cattle which you and Harris bought, and you told me there was money here to meet it. I thought you were all right, of course, and I did not come to town until to-day. Now the cashier says there is not a cursèd cent here to the credit of you and Harris."

The blood faded out of the cattle-shipper's face, leaving him as white as a sheet. He turned slowly to the cashier: "What became of that money?" he gasped.

"Why," the officer replied, "it was drawn out on the check of yourself and Harris. Did n't you know about it? The check was properly endorsed."

"Show me the check," said Thomas Woodford, striving hard to control the trembling of his voice. "There must be some mistake."

The cashier went to his desk and returned with a check, which he spread out on the table before the cattle-shipper. The man seized it and carried it to the light, where he scrutinized it closely. It was in proper form and drawn in the firm name of "Woodford & Harris," directing the Fourth National Bank to pay to William Harris ten thousand dollars. It was properly endorsed by William Harris and bore the stamp of the New York Clearing House.

"When was this check cashed?" asked Woodford.

"It was sent in yesterday," answered the cashier. "Is there anything wrong with it?"

For a time Woodford did not speak. He stood with his back to the two men and was evidently attempting to arrive at some solution of the matter. Presently he turned and faced the angry land-owner.

"There has been a mistake here, Mr. Izzard," he said, speaking slowly and calmly. "Suppose I give you my note for the money; the bank here will discount it, and you will not be put to any inconvenience."

To this the old gentleman readily assented. "All I want," he assured the shipper, "is to be safe. Your note, Woodford, is good for ten times the sum."

Thomas Woodford turned to the desk and drew a negotiable note for the amount of the check. This he gave to Mr. Izzard, and then hurried to the telegraph office, where he wired Harris asking for an immediate explanation of the mysterious transaction.

He was a man accustomed to keep his own counsels, and he was not yet ready to abandon them. He gave directions where the answer was to be sent, then he went to the hotel, locked himself in his room, and began to pace the floor, striving to solve the enigma of this queer proceeding on the part of William Harris.

The transaction had an ugly appearance. The money had been placed in the bank by the two men for the express purpose of meeting this check, which he had given to Izzard as a part payment on his stock. Harris knew this perfectly, and had suggested it. Now, how should it happen that he had drawn the money in his own name almost immediately upon his arrival in New York?

Could it be that Harris had concluded to steal the money? This the cattle-shipper refused to believe. He had known Harris for years, and knew that he was considered honest, as the world goes. Besides, Harris would not dare to make such a bold move for the purpose of robbery. His name was on the back of the check; there was no apparent attempt to conceal it. No, there could be but one explanation, considered Woodford: Harris had found the market rising and a great opportunity to make a vast sum of money; consequently he had bought more stock and had been compelled to use this money for the purpose of payment. There could be no other explanation, so the cattle-shipper convinced himself.

Thomas Woodford was not a man of wavering decisions. When his conclusion was once formed, that was the end of it. He went over to the wash-stand, bathed his face, and turned to leave the room. As he did so, some one rapped on the door; when he opened it, a messenger boy handed him a telegram. He took the message, closed the door, and went over to the window. For a moment the dread of what the little yellow envelope might possibly contain, made the big rough cattle-shipper tremble. Then he dismissed the premonition as an unreasonable fear, and with calm finger opened the message. The telegram was from New York, and contained these few words: "Have been robbed. Everything is lost," and was signed "William Harris."

Thomas Woodford staggered as if some one had dealt him a terrible blow in the face. The paper fell from his fingers and fluttered down on the floor. The room appeared to swim round him; his heart thumped violently for a moment, and then seemed to die down in his breast and cease its beating. He sank down in his chair and fell forward on the table, his big body limp under the shock of this awful calamity. It was all perfectly plain to him now. The entire transaction from the beginning to the end had been a deep-laid, cunning plan to rob him. The checking out of the ten thousand dollars was but a small part of it Harris had sold the cattle, and, seeking to keep the money, had simply said that he had been robbed. The story about the probable dissolution of the exporters' combine had been all a lie. He had been the dupe—the easy, willing dupe, of a cunning villain.

William Harris had come to West Virginia with the deliberate intention of inveigling him into this very trap. He had left New York with the entire scheme well planned. He had stopped at Bridgeport and told him the plausible story about what would happen to the combine, in order to arouse his interest and draw him into the plot and to account for his own presence in the cattle region. It was a shrewdly constructed tale, which, under the circumstances, the most cautious man in the business would have believed.

The man winced as he recalled how cunningly Harris had forced him to do the very things he desired done, without appearing to even suggest them. There was the deposit of the fund in the partnership name,—that seemed all reasonable enough. It had not occurred to him that this money would then be subject to Harris's check as well as his own. Then, too, it was reasonable that he should go out and buy the cattle, and Harris ship them,—Harris was a commission-merchant by trade, and this division of the work was natural. Such a robbery had not occurred before in all the history of this business, and how fatally well all the circumstances and the customs of the trade fitted into the plan of this daring rascal!

Then, like a benumbing ache, came the gradual appreciation of the magnitude of this loss. The cattle were worth twenty thousand dollars. He had agreed to pay Izzard that sum for the drove, and then there was the five thousand of his own money. Twenty-five thousand dollars in all. It was no small sum for the wealthiest to lose, and to this man in his despair it loomed large indeed.

Financial ruin is an evil-featured demon at best. The grasp of his hand is blighting; the leer of his sunken face, maddening. It requires strong will to face the monster when one knows that he is coming, even after his shadow has been flitting across one's path for years. When he leaps down suddenly from the dark upon the shoulders of the unsuspecting passer-by, that one must be strong indeed if all that he possesses of virtue and honesty and good motive be not driven out from him.

The old clock on the court-house struck five, its battered iron tongue crying out from above the place where men were accustomed to resort for Justice.

The sound startled Woodford and reminded him of something. He arose and went to the window and stood looking at the gaunt old building.

Yes, there was the Law. He had almost forgotten that, and the Law would not tolerate wrong. It hated the evil-doer, and hunted him down even to the death, and punished him. Men were often weak and half blind, but the Law was strong always, and its eyes were far-sighted. The world was not so large that the rogue could hide from it. In its strength it would seek him out and hold him responsible for the evil he had done. It stood ever in its majesty between the knave and those upon whom he sought to prey; its shadow, heavy with warning, lay always before the faces of vicious men.

In his bitterness, Woodford thanked Heaven that this was true. From the iron hand of the Law; William Harris should have vengeance visited upon him to the very rim of the measure.

VI.

Randolph Mason looked up from his desk as William Harris burst into his office. The commission-merchant's face was red, and he was panting with excitement. "Mr. Mason," he cried, "there is trouble on foot; you must help me out!"

"Trouble," echoed Mason, "is it any new thing to meet? Why do you come back with your petty matters?"

"It is no petty matter, sir," said Harris; "you planned the whole thing for me, and you said it was no crime. Now they are trying to put me in the penitentiary. You must have been wrong when you said it was no crime."

"Wrong?" said Mason, sharply. "What fool says I am wrong?"

"Why, sir," continued Harris, rapidly, "Thomas Woodford has applied to the Governor for an extradition, asking that I be turned over to the authorities of West Virginia on the charge of having committed a felony. You said I could draw out the partnership fund and keep it, and that I could sell the cattle and buy foreign exchange with the money, and it would be no crime. Now they are after me, and you must go to Albany and see about it."

"I shall not go to Albany," said Mason. "You have committed no crime and cannot be punished."

"But," said Harris, anxiously, "won't they take me down there? Won't the Governor turn me over to them?"

"The Governor," continued Mason, "is no fool. The affidavit stating the facts, which must accompany the application, will show on its face that no crime has been committed. You were a partner, with a partner's control of the funds. The taking of partnership property by one partner is no crime. Neither did you steal the cattle. They were sold to you. Your partner trusted you. If you do not pay, it is his misfortune. It was all a business affair, and by no possible construction can be twisted into a crime. Nor does it matter how the partnership was formed, so that it existed. It is no crime to lie in regard to an opinion. You have violated no law,—you have simply taken advantage of its weak places to your own gain and to the hurt of certain stupid fools. The Attorney General will never permit an extradition in this case while the world stands. Go home, man, and sleep,—you are as safe from the law as though you were in the grave."

With that, Randolph Mason arose and opened the office door. "I bid you good-morning, sir," he said curtly.

The Governor of New York pushed the papers across the table to the Attorney General. "I would like you to look at this application for the extradition of one Harris, charged with committing a felony in the State of West Virginia," he said. "The paper seems to be regular, but I am somewhat in doubt as to the proper construction to be placed upon the affidavit stating the facts alleged to constitute this crime."

VII.

The Attorney General took the papers and went over them rapidly. "Well," he said, "there is nothing wrong with the application. Everything is regular except the affidavit, and it is quite clear that it fails to support this charge of felony."

"I was inclined to that opinion," said the Governor, "and I thought best to submit the matter to you."

"It is usual," continued the Attorney General, "to grant the application without question, where the papers are regular and the crime is charged, and it is not required that the crime be charged with the legal exactness necessary in an indictment. The Governor is not permitted to try the question whether the accused is guilty or not guilty. Nor is he to be controlled by the question whether the offence is or is not a crime in his own State, the question before him being whether the act is punishable as a crime in the demanding State. The Governor cannot go behind the face of the papers nor behind the facts alleged to constitute a crime, and if these facts, by any reasonable construction, support the charge of crime, the extradition will usually be granted. But it is a solemn proceeding, and one not to be trifled with, and not to be invoked without good cause, nor to be used for the purpose of redressing civil injuries, or for the purpose of harassing the citizens; and where on the face of the affidavit it is plainly evident that no crime has been committed, and that by no possible construction of the facts stated could the matter be punishable as a crime, then it is the duty of the Governor to refuse the extradition.

"In this case the authorities in the demanding State have filed an affidavit setting forth at length the facts alleged to constitute a felony. This paper shows substantially that a general partnership was formed by William Harris and Thomas Woodford, and that pursuant to such business relations certain partnership property came into the possession of Harris; this property he converted to his own use. It is clear that this act constituted no crime under the statutes of West Virginia or the common law there obtaining. The property was general partnership property; the money taken was a general partnership fund, subject to the check of either partner. The partner Harris was properly in possession of the cattle as a part owner. He was also lawfully entitled to the possession of the partnership fund if he saw fit to draw it out and use it. If it be presumed that his story of the robbery is false, and that he deliberately planned to secure possession of the property and money, and did so secure possession of it, and converted it to his own use, yet he has committed no crime. He has simply taken advantage of the trust reposed in him by his partner Woodford, and has done none of those acts essential to a felony. The application must be refused."

"That was my opinion," said the Governor, "but such a great wrong had been done that I hesitated to refuse the extradition."

"Yes," answered the Attorney General, "all the wrong of a serious felony has been done, but no crime has been committed. The machinery of criminal jurisprudence cannot be used for the purpose of redressing civil wrong, the distinction being that, by a fiction of law, crimes are wrongs against the State, and in order to be a crime the offence must be one of those wrongs described by the law as being against the peace and dignity of the State. If, on the other hand, the act be simply a wrong to the citizen and not of the class described as being offences against the State, it is no crime, no matter how injurious it may be or how wrongful to the individual. The entire transaction was a civil matter resulting in injury to the citizen, Woodford, but it is no crime, and is not the proper subject of an extradition."

The Governor turned around in his chair. "James," he said to his private secretary, "return the application for the extradition of William Harris, and say that upon the face of the papers it is plainly evident that no crime has been committed."

The blow which Fate had sought to deliver with such malicious cunning against the confidential clerk of Beaumont, Milton, & Company had been turned aside, and had fallen with all its crushing weight upon the shoulders of another man, five hundred miles to westward, within the jurisdiction of a distant commonwealth.

IV—THE ERROR OF WILLIAM VAN BROOM

[The lawyer will at once see that the false making of this paper is no forgery, and that no crime has been committed. See the Virginia case of Foulke in 2 Robinson's Virginia Reports, 836; the case of Jackson vs. Weisiger, 11 Ky. (Monroe Reports), 214; and the later case of Charles Waterman vs. The People, 67 Ill., 91.]

I.

THE morning paper contained this extravagant personal: "Do not suicide. If you are a non-resident of New York in difficulty, at nine to-night walk east by the corner of the —————— Building with a copy of this paper in your right hand."

The conservative foreigner, unfamiliar with our great dailies, would, perhaps, be surprised that the editor would print such a questionable announcement in his paper, but at this time in New York the personal column had become a very questionable directory, resorted to by all classes of mankind for every conceivable purpose, be it gain, adventure, or even crime; no one thought to question the propriety of such publications. Indeed, no one stopped to consider them at all, unless he happened to be a party in interest.

II.

Afew minutes before the hour mentioned in the above personal, a cab came rattling down ——————

Street. The driver wore a fur-cap and a great-coat buttoned up around his ears. As he turned the corner to the —————— Building, he glanced down at his front wheel and brought his horses up with a jerk. There was evidently something wrong with the wheel, for he jumped down from the box to examine it. He shook the wheel, took off the tap, and began to move the hub carefully out toward the end of the axle. As he worked he kept his eyes on the corner. Presently a big, plainly dressed man walked slowly down by the building. He carried a half-open newspaper in his right hand and seemed to be keeping a sharp lookout around him. He stopped for a moment by the carriage, satisfied himself that it was empty, and went on. At the next corner he climbed up on the seat of the waiting patrol wagon and disappeared.

The cabman seemed to be engrossed with the repair of his wheel and gave no indication that he had seen the stranger. Almost immediately thereafter a second man passed the corner with a newspaper in prominent evidence. He was a "hobo" of the most pronounced type and marched by with great difficulty. After he had passed, he turned round and threw the newspaper into the gutter with a volley of curses.

The cabman worked on at his wheel. He had now removed it to the end of the axle and was scraping the boxing with his knife. At this moment a young man wearing a gray overcoat and a gray slouch hat came rapidly down the street. At the corner he put his hand quickly into his overcoat pocket, took out a newspaper, and immediately thrust it into his other pocket. The cabman darted across the street and touched him on the shoulder. The man turned with a quick, nervous start. The cabman took off his cap, said something in a low tone, and pointed to his wheel. The two men crossed to the carriage. The cabman held the axle and the stranger slipped the wheel into place, while the two talked in low tones. When it was done, the stranger turned round, stepped up on the pavement, and hurried on by the building. The cabman shut his door with a bang, climbed up on his box, and drove rapidly down ———— Street.

III.

Parks," said Randolph Mason, taking off his great-coat in the private office, "who wanted to see me at this unusual hour?"

"He was a Philadelphia man, he said, sir," answered the little melancholy clerk.

"Well," said Mason, sharply, "did he expect to die before morning that I should be sent for in the middle of the night?"

"He said that he would leave at six, sir, and must see you as soon as possible, so I thought I had best send for you."

"He is to be here at ten, you say?"

"At ten, sir," answered the little man, going out into the other office and closing the door behind him. When the door was closed, Parks went over to a corner of the room, took up a hackman's overcoat and fur cap, put them into one of the bookcases and locked the sliding top. Then he went quietly out of the room and down the steps to the entrance of the building.

In the private office Randolph Mason walked backward and forward with his hands in his pockets. He was restless and his eyes were bright.

"Another weakling," he muttered, "making puny efforts to escape from Fate's trap, or seeking to slip from under some gin set by his fellows. Surely, the want of resources on the part of the race is utter, is abysmal. What miserable puppets men are! moved backward and forward in Fate's games as though they were strung on a wire and had their bellies filled with sawdust! Yet each one has his problem, and that is the important matter. In these problems one pits himself against the mysterious intelligence of Chance,—against the dread cunning and the fatal patience of Destiny. Ah! these are worthy foemen. The steel grates when one crosses swords with such mighty fencers."

There was a sound as of men conversing in low tones in the outer office. Mason stopped short and turned to the door. As he did so, the door was opened from the outside and a man entered, closed the door behind him, and remained standing with his back against it.

Randolph Mason looked down at the stranger sharply. The man wore a gray suit and gray overcoat; he was about twenty-five, of medium height, with a clean-cut, intelligent face that was peculiar; originally it had expressed an indulgent character of unusual energy. Now it could not be read at all. It was simply that silent, immobile mask so sought after by the high-grade criminal. His face was white, and the perspiration, was standing out on his forehead, indicating that he was laboring under some deep and violent emotion. Yet, with all, his manner was composed and deliberate, and his face gave no sign other than its whiteness; it was calm and expressionless, as the face of the dead.

Randolph Mason dragged a big chair up to his desk, sat down in his office chair and pointed to the other. The stranger came and sat down in the big chair, gripping its arms with his hands, and without introduction or comment began to talk in a jerky, metallic voice.

"This is all waste of time," he said. "You won't help me. There is no reason for my being here. I should have had it over by this time, and yet that would not help her, and she is the only one. It would be the meanest kind of cowardice to leave her to suffer; and yet I dare not live to see her suffer, I could not bear that. I love her too much for that, I——"

"Sir," said Mason, brutally, "this is all irrelevant rant. Come to the point of your difficulty."

The stranger straightened up and passed his hand across his forehead. "Yes," he said, "you are right, sir; it is all rant. I forget where I am. I will be as brief and concise as possible.

"My name is Camden Gerard. I am a gambler by profession. My mother died when I was about ten years old and my father, then a Philadelphia lawyer, found himself with two children, myself and my little sister, a mere baby in arms. He sent me to one of the eastern colleges and put the baby in a convent. Thus things ran on for perhaps ten or twelve years. The evil effect of forcing me into a big college at an early age soon became apparent I came under the influence of a rapid and unscrupulous class and soon became as rapid and unscrupulous as the worst. I went all the paces and gradually became an expert college gambler of such high order that I was able to maintain myself. At about twelve my sister Marie began to show remarkable talent as an artist and my father, following her wishes, took her to Paris and placed her in one of the best art schools of that city. In a short time thereafter my father died suddenly, and it developed after investigation that he had left no estate whatever. I sold the books and other personal effects, and found myself adrift in the world with a few hundred dollars, no business, no profession, and no visible means of support, and, further, I had this helpless child to look after.

"I went to supposed friends of my father and asked them to help me into some business by which I could maintain myself and my little sister. They promised, but put me off with one excuse after another, until I finally saw through their hypocrisy and knew that they never intended to assist me. I felt, indeed, that I was adrift, utterly helpless and friendless, and the result was, that I resorted to my skill as a gambler for the purpose of making a livelihood. For a time fortune favored me, and I lived well, and paid all the college expenses of Marie. I was proud of the child. She was sweet and lovable, and developing into a remarkably handsome girl. About two months ago, my luck turned sharply against me; everything went wrong with long jumps. Night after night I was beaten. Anybody broke me, even the 'tender-feet,' I gathered together every dollar possible and struggled against my bad fortune, but to no purpose. I only lost night after night. In the midst of all, Marie wrote to me for money to pay her quarterly bills. I replied that I would send it in a short time. I pawned everything, begged and borrowed and struggled, and resorted to every trick and resource of my craft; but all was utterly vain and useless. I was penniless and stranded. On the heels of it all, I to-day received another letter from Marie, saying that her bills must be paid by the end of the month, or they would turn her out into the city."

His voice trembled and the perspiration poured out on his forehead. "You know what it means for a helpless young girl to be turned out in Paris," he went on; "I know, and the thought of it makes me insanely desperate. Now," said the man, looking Mason squarely in the eyes, "I have told you all the truth. What am I to do?"

For a time Mason's face took on an air of deep abstraction. "This is Saturday night," he said, as though talking to himself. "You should complete it by Friday. There is time enough."

"Young man," he continued, speaking clearly and precisely, "you are to leave New York for West Virginia to-morrow morning. A messenger boy will meet you at the train, with a package of papers which I shall send. In it you will find full instructions and such things as you will need. These instructions you are to follow to the very letter. Everything will depend on doing exactly as I say, but," he continued, with positive and deliberate emphasis, "this must not fail."

The man arose and drew a deep breath. "It will not fail," he said; "I will do anything to save her from disgrace,—anything." Then he went out.

At the entrance of the building Parks stepped up and touched the stranger on the shoulder. "My friend," he said, "I will bring those papers myself, and I will see that you have sufficient money to carry this thing through. But remember that I am not to be trifled with. You are to come here just as soon as you return."

IV.

Shortly before noon on Monday morning, Camden Gerard stepped into the jewelry establishment of William Van Broom, in the city of Wheeling, and asked for the proprietor. That gentleman came forward in no very kindly humor. Upon seeing the well dressed young man, he at once concluded that he was a high-grade jewel drummer, and being a practical business man, he was kindly at sales and surly at purchases.

"This is Mr. Van Broom, I believe," said the young man. "My name is

Gerard. I am from New York, sir." Then noticing the jeweller's expression, he added, quickly: "I am not a salesman, sir, and am not going to consume your time. I am in West Virginia on business, and stepped in here to present a letter of introduction which my friend, Bartholdi, insisted upon writing."

The affability of the jeweller returned with a surge. He bowed and beamed sweetly as he broke the seal of the letter of introduction. The paper bore the artistic stamp of Bartholdi and Banks, the great diamond importers, and ran as follows:

"William Van Broom, Esq.,

"Wheeling, West Va.

"Dear Sir:

"This will introduce Mr. Camden Gerard. Kindly show him every possible courtesy, for which we shall be under the greatest obligations.

"Most sincerely your obedient servants,

"Bartholdi and Banks"

The jeweller's eyes opened wide with wonder. He knew this firm to be the largest and most aristocratic dealers in the world. It was much honor, and perhaps vast benefit, to be of service to them, and he was flattered into the seventh heaven.

"I am indeed glad to meet you, sir," he said, seizing the man's hand and shaking it vigorously. "I certainly hope that I can be of service. It is now near twelve; you will come with me to lunch at the club?"

"I thank you very much," answered Camden Gerard, "but I am compelled to go to the Sistersville oil field on the noon train. However, I will return at eight, and shall expect you to dine with me at the hotel."

The jeweller accepted the invitation with ill-concealed delight. The young man thanked him warmly for his kindly interest, bade him good-day, and went out.

That night at eight, Camden Gerard and Mr. William Van Broom dined in the best style the city could afford. The wine was excellent and plentiful, and Gerard proved to be most entertaining. He was brilliant and considerate to such a degree, that when the two men parted for the night the jeweller assured himself that he had never met a more delightful companion.

The following morning Camden Gerard dropped into the store for a few moments, and while conversing with his friend Van Broom, noticed a little ring in the show window. He remarked on its beauty, and intimated that he must purchase a birthday present for his little daughter. The jeweller took the ring from the case and handed it to Gerard. That gentleman discovered that it was far prettier than he had at first imagined it, and inquired the price.

"It is marked at twenty-five dollars," said the jeweller.

"Why," said Camden Gerard, "that is very cheap; I will take it."

The jeweller wrapped up the ring and gave it to the New Yorker. That gentleman paid the money and returned to his hotel.

The next day Camden Gerard was presumably down in the great Tyler County oil field. At any rate he returned to the city on the evening train and dined with Van Broom at the club. As the evening waned, the men grew confidential. Gerard spoke of the vast fortunes that were made in oil. He said that the West Virginia fields were scarce half developed, but that they had already attracted the attention of the great Russian companies and that gigantic operations might be soon expected. He denounced the autocratic policy of the Czar in regard to oil transportation, and hinted vaguely at vast international combines. He spoke of St. Petersburg and the larger Russian cities; of the manners and customs of the nobility; of their vast fortunes, and their very great desire to invest in America. He intimated vaguely that there now existed in New York a colossal syndicate backed by unlimited Russian capital, but he gave the now excited and curious jeweller no definite information concerning himself or his business in West Virginia, shrewdly leaving Van Broom to draw his own inferences.

It was late when William Van Broom retired to his residence. He was happy and flattered, and with reason. Had he not been selected by the great firm of Bartholdi & Banks to counsel with one who, he strongly suspected, was the private agent of princes?

About two o'clock on the following Thursday afternoon, Mr. Camden Gerard called upon William Van Broom and said that he wished to speak with him in his private office. The New Yorker was soiled and grimy, and had evidently just come from a train, but he was smiling and in high spirits.

When the two men were alone in the private office, Camden Gerard took a roll of paper from his pocket, and turned to Van Broom. "Here are some papers," he said, speaking low that he might not be overheard. "I have no secure place to put them, and I would be under great obligations to you if you would kindly lock them up in your safe."

"Certainly," said the jeweller, taking the papers and crossing to the safe. He threw back the door and pulled out one of the little boxes. It contained an open leather case in which there was a magnificent diamond necklace.

"By George!" said Camden Gerard, "those are splendid stones."

"Yes," answered Van Broom, taking out the case and handing it to the New Yorker. "They are too valuable for my trade; I am going to return them."

Camden Gerard carried the necklace to the light and examined it critically. The stones were not large but they were clear and flawless.

"What are these worth?" he said, turning to Van Broom.

"Thirty-five hundred dollars," answered the jeweller.

"What!" cried Gerard, "only thirty-five hundred dollars for this necklace? It is the cheapest thing I ever saw. You are away under the foreign dealers."

"They are cheap," said Van Broom. "That is almost the wholesale price."

"But," said Camden Gerard, "you must be mistaken. Your mark is certainly wrong. I have seen smaller stones in the Russian shops for double the price."

"We can't sell the necklace at that figure," said Van Broom, smiling. "We are not such sharks as your foreign dealers."

"If you mean that," said Camden Gerard, "I will buy these jewels here and now. I had intended purchasing something in the east for my wife, but I can never do better than this."

The New Yorker took out his pocket-book and handed Van Broom a bill. "Before you retract," he said, "here is fifty to seal the bargain. Get your hat and come with me to the bank."

"All right," said Mr. Van Broom, taking the money. "The necklace is yours, my friend." Camden Gerard closed the leather case and put it into his pocket. The jeweller locked the safe, put on his hat, and the two went out of the store and down the street to the banking house of the Mechanics' Trust Company. Mr. Gerard enquired for the cashier. The teller informed him that the cashier was in the back room of the bank and if he would step back he could see him. The New Yorker asked his companion to wait for a moment until he spoke with the cashier. Then he went back into the room indicated by the teller, closing the door after him.

The cashier sat at a table engaged with a pile of correspondence. He was busy and looked up sharply as the man entered.

"Sir," said the New Yorker, "have you received a sealed package from the Adams Express Company consigned to one Camden Gerard?"

"No," answered the cashier, turning to his work.

"You have not?" repeated Gerard, excitedly, "then I will run down to the telegraph office and see what is the matter." Thereupon he crossed hurriedly to the side door of the office, opened it and stepped out into the street. The cashier went on with his work.

For perhaps a quarter of an hour William Van Broom waited for his companion to conclude his business with the cashier. Finally he grew impatient and asked the teller to remind Mr. Gerard that he was waiting. The teller returned in a moment and said that the gentleman had gone to the telegraph office some time ago. The jeweller's heart dropped like a lead plummet. He turned without a word and hurried to the office of the Western Union. Here his fears were confirmed, Camden Gerard had not been in the office. He ran across the street to the hotel and enquired for the New Yorker. The clerk informed him that the gentleman had paid his bill and left the hotel that morning. The jeweller's anxiety was at fever heat, but with all he was a man of business method and knew the very great value of silence. He called a carriage, went to the chief of police, and set his machinery in motion. Returning to his place of business he opened the safe and took out the package of papers which Camden Gerard had given him. Upon examination this proved to be simply a roll of blank oil leases. Then remembering the letter of introduction, he telegraphed to Bartholdi & Banks. Hours passed and not the slightest trace of Camden Gerard could be found. The presumed friend of the great diamond importers had literally vanished from the face of the earth.

About four o'clock the jeweller received an answer from Bartholdi & Banks, stating that they knew no such man as Camden Gerard and that his letter of introduction was false. Mr. William Van Broom was white with despair. He put the letter and answer into his pocket and went at once to the office of the prosecuting attorney for the State and laid the whole matter before him.

"My dear sir," said that official, when Mr. Van Broom had finished his story, "your very good friend Camden Gerard owes you thirty-four hundred and fifty dollars, which he will perhaps continue to owe. You may as well go back to your business."

"What do you mean?" said the jeweller.

"I mean," replied the attorney, "that you have been the dupe of a shrewd knave who is familiar with the weak places in the law and has resorted to an ingenious scheme to secure possession of your property without rendering himself liable to criminal procedure. It is true that if the diamonds were located you could attach and recover them by a civil suit, but it is scarcely possible that such a shrewd knave would permit himself to be caught with the jewels, and it is certain that he has some reasonably safe method by which he can dispose of them without fear of detection. He has trapped you and has committed no crime. If you had the fellow in custody now, the judge would release him the moment an application was made. The entire matter was only a sale. He bought the jewels and you trusted him. He is no more a law-breaker than you are. He is only a sharper dealer."

"But, sir," cried the angry Van Broom, spreading the false letter out on the table, "that is forged, every word of it. I will send this fellow to the penitentiary for forgery. I will spend a thousand dollars to catch him."

"If you should spend a thousand dollars to catch him," said the attorney, smiling, "you would never be able to send him to the penitentiary on that paper. It is not forgery."

"Not forgery!" shouted the jeweller, "not forgery, man! The rascal wrote every word of that letter. He signed the name of Bartholdi & Banks at the bottom of it. Every word of that paper is false. The company never heard of it. Here is their telegram."

"Mr. Van Broom," said the public prosecutor, "listen to me, sir. All that you say is perhaps true. Camden Gerard doubtless wrote the entire paper and signed the name of Bartholdi & Banks, and presented it to you for a definite purpose. To such an act men commonly apply the term forgery, and in the common acceptation of the word it is forgery and a reprehensible wrong; but legally, the false making of such a paper as this is not forgery and is no crime. In order to constitute the crime of forgery, the instrument falsely made must be apparently capable of effecting a fraud, of being used to the prejudice of another's right. It must be such as might be of legal efficacy, or might be the foundation of some legal liability.

"This paper in question, although falsely made, has none of the vital elements of forgery under the law. If genuine, it would have no legal validity, as it affects no legal rights. It would merely be an attempt to receive courtesies on a promise, of no legal obligation, to reciprocate them; and courtesies have never been held to be the subject of legal fraud. This is a mere letter of introduction, which, by no possibility, could subject the supposed writer to any pecuniary loss or legal liability. It is not a subject of forgery, and its false making is no crime.

"Men commonly believe that all writings falsely made or falsely altered are forgeries. There was never a greater error. Forgery may be committed only of those instruments in writing which, if genuine, would, or might appear as the foundation of another man's liability, or the evidence of his right. All wrongful and injurious acts are not punished by the law. Wrongs to become crimes must measure up to certain definite and technical standards. These standards are laid down rigidly by the law and cannot be contracted or expanded. They are fixed and immutable. The act done must fit closely into the prescribed measure, else it is no crime. If it falls short, never so little, in any one vital element, the law must, and will, disregard it as criminal, no matter how injurious, or wrongful, or unjust it may be. The law is a rigid and exact science."

Mr. William Van Broom dropped his hands to his sides and gazed at the lawyer in wonder.

"These facts," continued the attorney, in his clear, passionless voice, "are matters of amazement to the common people when brought to their attention. They fail to see the wise but technical distinctions. They are willing to trust to what they are pleased to call common-sense, and, falling into traps laid by the cunning villain, denounce the law for impotency."

"Well," said the jeweller, as he arose and put on his overcoat, "what is the good of the law anyhow?"

The prosecuting attorney smiled wearily. To him the wisdom of the law was clear, beautiful, and superlatively just. To the muddy-headed tradesman it was as color to the blind.

V.

Over in the art school of old Monsieur Pontique, Marie Gerard saw the result of the entire matter in the light of kindness and sweet self-sacrifice; and perhaps she saw it as it was. This is a queer world indeed.

V—THE MEN OF THE JIMMY

[See Ranney vs. The People, 22 N.Y.R., 413; Scott vs. The People, 66 Barb. [N.Y], 62; The People vs. Blanchard, 90 N. Y. Repts., 314. Also, Rex vs. Douglas, 2 Russell on Crimes, 624, and other cases there cited.]

I.

PARKS," said Randolph Mason, "has Leslie Wilder a country place on the Hudson?"

"Yes, sir," replied the bald little clerk. "It is at Cliphmore, I think, sir."

"Well," said Mason, "here is his message, Parks, asking that I come to him immediately. It seems urgent and probably means a will. Find out what time a train leaves the city and have a carriage."

The clerk took the telegram, put on his coat, and went down on the street. It was cold and snowing heavily. The wind blew up from the river, driving the snow in great, blinding sheets. The melancholy Parks pulled his hat down over his face, walked slowly round the square, and came back to the entrance of the office building. Instead of taking the elevator he went slowly up the steps into the outer office. Here he took off his coat and went over to the window, and stood for some minutes looking out at the white city.

"At any rate he will not suspect me," he muttered, "and we must get every dollar possible while we can. He won't last always."

At this moment a carriage drove up and stopped by the curb. Parks turned round quickly and went into Mason's private office. "Sir," he said, "your train leaves at six ten, and the carriage is waiting."

When Randolph Mason stepped from the train at the little Cliphmore station, it was pitch dark, and the snow was sweeping past in great waves. He groped his way to the little station-house and pounded on the door. There was no response. As he turned round a man stepped up on the platform, pulled off his cap, and said, "Excuse me, sir, the carriage is over here, sir." Mason followed the man across the platform, and up what seemed to be a gravel road for perhaps twenty yards. Here they found a closed carriage. The man threw open the door, helped Mason in, and closed it, forcing the handle carefully. Then he climbed up in front, struck the horses, and drove away.

For perhaps half an hour the carriage rattled along the gravel road, and

Mason sat motionless. Suddenly he leaned over, turned the handle of the carriage door, and jerked it sharply. The door did not open. He tucked the robes around him and leaned back in the seat, like a man who had convinced himself of the truth of something that he suspected. Presently the carriage began to wobble and jolt as though upon an unkept country road. The driver pulled up his horses and allowed them to walk. The snow drifted up around him and he seemed to have great difficulty in keeping to the road Presently he stopped, climbed down from the box and attempted to open the door. He apparently had some difficulty, but finally threw it back and said: "Dis is de place, sir."

Randolph Mason got out and looked around him. "This may be the place," he said to the man, "but this is not Wilder's.'"

"I said dis here is de place," answered the man, doggedly.

"Beyond a doubt," said Mason, "and since you are such a cunning liar I will go in."

The driver left the horses standing and led the way across what seemed to be an unkept lawn, Mason following. A house loomed up in the dark before them. The driver stopped and rapped on the door. There was no light visible and no indication of any inhabitant. The driver rapped again without getting any response. Then he began to curse, and to kick the door violently.

"Will you be quiet?" said a voice from the inside, and the door opened. The hall-way was dark, and the men on the outside could not see the speaker.

"Here is de man, sir," said the driver.

"That is good," replied the voice; "come in."

The two men stepped into the house. The man who had bid them enter closed the door and bolted it. Then he took a lantern from under his coat and led them back through the hall to the rear of the building. The house was dilapidated and old, and had the appearance of having been deserted for many years.

The man with the lantern turned down a side hall, opened a door, and ushered Mason into a big room, where there was a monster log fire blazing.

This room was dirty and bare. The windows were carefully covered from the inside, so as to prevent the light from being seen. There was no furniture except a broken table and a few old chairs. At the table sat an old man smoking a pipe. He had on a cap and overcoat, and was studying a newspaper spread out before him. He seemed to be spelling out the words with great difficulty, and did not look up. Randolph Mason took off his great-coat, threw it over a chair, and seated himself before the fire. The man with the lantern placed it on the mantel-shelf, took up a short pipe, and seating himself on a box by the hearth corner, began to smoke. He was a powerful man, perhaps forty years old, clean and decently dressed. His forehead was broad. His eyes were unusually big and blue. He seemed to be of considerable intelligence, and his expression, taken all in all, was innocent and kindly.

For a time there was nothing said. The driver went out to look after his horses. The old man at the table labored on at his newspaper, and Randolph Mason sat looking into the fire. Suddenly he turned to the man at his left. "Sir," said he "to what difficulty am I indebted for this honor?"

"Well," said the man, putting his pipe into his pocket, "the combination is too high for us this time; we can't crack it. We knew about you and sent for you."

"Your plan for getting me here does little credit to your wits," said Mason; "the trick is infantile and trite."

"But it got you here anyhow," replied the man.

"Yes," said Mason, "when the dupe is willing to be one. But suppose I had rather concluded to break with your driver at the station? It is likewise dangerous to drive a man locked in a carriage when he may easily kill you through the window."

"Trow on de light, Barker," said the old man at the table; "what is de use of gropin'?"

"Well," said the younger man, "the fact is simply this: The Boss and Leary and a 'supe' were cracking a safe out in the States. They were tunnelling up early in the morning, when the 'supe' forced a jimmy through the floor. The bank janitor saw it, and they were all caught and sent up for ten years. We have tried every way to get the boys out, but have been unable to do anything at all, until a few days ago we discovered that one of the guards could be bribed to pass in a kit, and to hit the 'supe' if there should be any shooting, if we could put up enough stuff. He was to be discharged at the end of his month anyway, and he did not care. But he would not move a finger under four thousand dollars. We have been two weeks trying to raise the money, and have now only twelve hundred. The guard has only a week longer, and another opportunity will not occur perhaps in a lifetime. We have tried everything, and cannot raise another hundred, and it is our only chance to save the Boss and Leary."

"Dat is right," put in the old man; "it don't go at all wid us, we is gittin' trowed on it, and dat is sure unless dis gent knows a good ting to push, and dat is what he is here fur, to name de good ting to push. Dat is right, dat 's what we 's got to have, and we 's got to have it now. We don't keer no hell-room fur de 'supe,' it's de Boss and Leary we wants."

Randolph Mason got up and stood with his back to the fire. The lines of his face grew deep and hard. Presently he thrust out his jaw, and began to walk backward and forward across the room.

"Barker," muttered the old man, looking up for the first time, "de guy has jimmy iron in him."

The blue-eyed man nodded and continued to watch Mason curiously. Suddenly, as he passed the old man at the table, Mason stopped short and put his finger down on the newspaper. The younger man leaped up noiselessly, and looking over Mason's shoulder read the head-lines under his finger. "Kidnapped," it ran. "The youngest son of Cornelius Rockham stolen from the millionaire's carriage. Large rewards offered. No clew."

"Do you know anything about this?" said Mason, shortly.

"Dat 's de hell," replied the old man, "we does n't."

Mason straightened up and swung round on his heel. "Sir," he said to the man Barker, "are you wanted in New York?"

"No," he replied, "I am just over; they don't know me."

"Good," said Mason, "it is as plain as a blue print. Come over here."

The two crossed to the far corner of the room. There Mason grasped the man by the shoulder and began to talk to him rapidly, but in a voice too low to be heard by the old man at the table. "Smoove guy, dis," muttered the old man. "He may be fly in de nut, but he takes no chances on de large audejence."

For perhaps twenty minutes Randolph Mason talked to the man at the wall. At first the fellow did not seem to understand, but after a time his face lighted up with wonder and eagerness, and his assurance seemed to convince the speaker, for presently they came back together to the fire.

"You," said Mason to the old man, "what is your name?"

"It cuts no ice about de label," replied the old man, pulling at his pipe. "Fur de purposes of dis seeyance I am de Jook of Marlbone."

"Well," said Mason, putting on his coat, "Mr. Barker will tell your lordship what you are to do."

The big blue-eyed man went out and presently returned with the carriage driver. "Mr. Mason," he said, "Bill will drive you to the train and you will be in New York by twelve."

"Remember," said Mason, savagely, turning around at the door, "it must be exactly as I have told you, word for word."

II

Itell you," said Cornelius Rockham, "it is the most remarkable proposition that I have ever heard."

"It is strange," replied the Police Chief, thoughtfully. "You say the fellow declared that he had a proposition to make in regard to the child, and that he refused to make it save in the presence of witnesses."

"Yes, he actually said that he would not speak with me alone or where he might be misunderstood, but that he would come here to-night at ten and State the matter to me and such reliable witnesses as I should see fit to have, not less than three in number; that a considerable sum of money might be required, and that I would do well to have it in readiness; that if I feared robbery or treachery, I should fill the house with policemen, and take any and every precaution that I thought necessary. In fact, he urged that I should have the most reliable men possible for witnesses, and as many as I desired, and that I must avail myself of every police protection in order that I might feel amply and thoroughly secure."

"Well," said the Police Chief, "if the fellow is not straight he is a fool. No living crook would ever make such a proposition."

"So I am convinced," replied Mr. Rockham. "The precautions he suggests certainly prove it. He places himself absolutely in our hands, and knows that if any crooked work should be attempted we have everything ready to thwart it; that there is nothing that he could accomplish, and he would only be placing himself helplessly in the grasp of the police. However, we will not fail to avail ourselves of his suggestion. You will see to it, Chief?"

"Yes," said the officer, rising and putting on his coat. "We will give him no possible chance. It is now five. I will send the men in an hour."

At ten o'clock that night, the palatial residence of Cornelius Rockham was in a state of complete police blockade. All the approaches were carefully guarded. The house itself, from the basement to the very roof, literally swarmed with the trusted spies of the police. The Chief felt indeed that his elaborate precautions were in a vast measure unnecessary. He was not a quick man, but he was careful after a ponderous method, and trusted much to precautionary safeguards.

Cornelius Rockham, the Chief, and two sergeants in citizen's dress, were waiting. Presently the bell rang and a servant ushered a man into the room. He was big and plainly dressed. His hair was brown and his eyes were blue, frank and kindly and his expression was pleasant and innocent, almost infantile.

"Good-evening, gentlemen," he said, "I believe I am here by appointment with Mr. Rockham."

"Yes," replied Cornelius Rockham, rising, "pray be seated, sir. I have asked these gentlemen to be present, as you suggested."

"Your time is valuable, no doubt," said the man, taking the proffered chair, "and I will consume as little of it as possible. My name is Barker. I am a comparative stranger in this city, and by pure accident am enabled to make the proposition which I am going to make. Your child has been missing now for several days, I believe, without any clew whatever. I do not know who kidnapped it, nor any of the circumstances. It is now half-past ten o'clock. I do not know where it is at this time, and I could not now take you to it. At eleven o'clock to-night, I shall know where it is, and I shall be able to take you to it. But I need money, and I must have five thousand dollars to compensate me for the information."

The man paused for a moment, and passed his hand across his forehead. "Now," he went on, "to be perfectly plain. I will not trust you, and you, of course, will not trust me. In order to insure good faith on both sides, I must ask that you pay me the money here, in the presence of these witnesses, then handcuff me to a police officer, and I will take you to the child at eleven o'clock. You may surround me with all the guards you think proper, and take every precaution to insure your safety and prevent my escape. You will pardon my extreme frankness, but business is business, and we all know that matters of this kind must be arranged beforehand. Men are too indifferent after they get what they want." Barker stopped short, and looked up frankly at the men around him.

Cornelius Rockham did not reply, but his white, haggard face lighted up hopefully. He beckoned to the Police Chief, and the two went into an adjoining room.

"What do you think?" said Rockham, turning to the officer.

"That man," replied the Chief, "means what he says, or else he is an insane fool, and he certainly bears no indication of the latter. It is evident that he will not open his mouth until he gets the money, for the reason that he is afraid that he will be ignored after the child is recovered. I do not believe there is any risk in paying him now, and doing as he says; because he cannot possibly escape when fastened to a sergeant, and if he proves to be a fake, or tries any crooked work, we will return the money to you and lock him up."

"I am inclined to agree with you," replied Rockham; "the man is eccentric and suspicious, but he certainly will not move until paid, and we have no charge as yet upon which to arrest him. Nor would it avail us anything if we did. There is little if any risk, and much probability of learning something of the boy. I will do it."

He went down to the far end of the hall and took a package of bills from a desk. Then the two men returned to the drawing-room.

"Sir," said Rockham to Barker, "I accept your proposition, here is the money, but you must consider yourself utterly in our hands. I am willing to trust you, but I am going to follow your suggestion."

"A contract is a contract," replied Barker, taking the money and counting it carefully. When he had satisfied himself that the amount was correct he thrust the roll of bills into his outside coat-pocket.

"It is now fifteen minutes until eleven," said the Police Chief, stepping up to Barker's chair, "and if you are ready we will go."

"I am ready," said the man, getting up.

The Police Chief took a pair of steel handcuffs from his pocket, locked one part of them carefully on Barker's left wrist and fastened the other to the right wrist of the sergeant. Then they went out of the house and down the steps to the carriages.

The Police Chief, Barker, and the sergeant climbed into the first carriage, and Mr. Rockham and the other officer into the second.

"Have your man drive to the Central Park entrance," said Barker to the Chief. The officer called to the driver and the carriages rolled away. At the west entrance to Central Park the men alighted.

"Now, gentlemen," said Barker, "we must walk west to the second corner and wait there until a cab passes from the east. The cab will be close curtained and will be drawn by a sorrel cob. As it passes you will dart out, seize the horse, and take possession of the cab. You will find the child in the cab, but I must insist for my own welfare, that you make every appearance of having me under arrest and in close custody."

The five men turned down the street in the direction indicated. Mr. Rockham and one of the officers in the front and the other two following with Barker between them. For a time they walked along in silence. Then the Police Chief took some cigars from his pocket, gave one to the sergeant, and offering them to Barker said, "Will you smoke, sir?"

"Not a cigar, I thank you," replied the man, "but if you will permit me I will light my pipe." The two men stopped. Barker took a short pipe and a pouch of tobacco from his pocket, filled the pipe and lighted it; as he was about to return the pouch to his coat pocket, an old apple-woman, hobbling past, caught the odor and stopped.

"Fur de love of Hivin, Mister," she drawled, "give me a pipe uv yer terbaccy?" Barker laughed, tossed her the pouch, and the three hurried on.

At the corner indicated the men stopped. The Police Chief examined the handcuffs carefully to see that they were all right; then they drew back in the shadow and waited for the cab. Eleven o'clock came and passed and the cab did not appear. Mr. Rockham paced the sidewalk nervously and the policemen gathered close around Barker.

At half-past eleven o'clock Barker straightened up, shrugged his shoulders, and turned to the Police Chief. "It is no use," he said, "they are not here and they never will come now."

"What!" cried the Police Chief savagely, "do you mean that we are fooled?"

"Yes," said Barker, "all of us. It is no use I tell you, the thing is over."

"It is not over with you, my man," growled the Chief. "Here, sergeant, get Mr. Rockham his money and let us lock this fellow up."

The sergeant turned and thrust his hand into Barker's outside coat-pocket, then his chin dropped and he turned white. "It is gone!" he muttered.

"Gone!" shouted Rockham; "search the rascal!"

The sergeant began to go carefully over the man. Suddenly he stopped. "Chief," he muttered, "it was in that tobacco pouch."

The Police Chief staggered back and spun round on his heel. "Angels of Hell!" he gasped, "it was a cute trick, and it threw us all, every one of us."

Rockham bounded forward and brought his hand down heavily on Barker's shoulder. "As for you, my fine fellow," he said, bitterly, "we have you all right and we will land you in Sing Sing."

Barker was silent. In the dark the men could not see that he was smiling.

III.

The court-room of Judge Walter P. Wright was filled with an interested audience of the greater and unpunished criminals of New York. The application of Barker for a *habeas corpus*, on the ground that he had committed no crime, had attracted wide attention. It was known that the facts were not disputed, and the proceeding was a matter of wonder.

Some days before, the case had been submitted to the learned judge. The attorneys for the People had not been anxious enough to be interested, and looked upon the application as a farce. The young man who appeared for Barker announced that he represented one Randolph Mason, a counsellor, and was present only for the purpose of asking that Barker be discharged, and for the further purpose of filing the brief of Mason in support of the application. He made no argument whatever, and had simply handed up the brief, which the attorneys for the People had not thought it worth their while to examine.

Barker sat in the dock, grim and confident. The attorneys for the commonwealth were listless. The audience was silent and attentive. It was a vital matter to them. If Barker had committed no crime, what a rich, untramped field was open. The Judge laid his hand upon the books piled up beside him and looked down at the bar.

"This proceeding," he began, "is upon the application of one Lemuel Barker for a writ of *habeas corpus*, asking that he be discharged from custody, upon the ground that he has committed no crime punishable at common law or under the statutes of New York. An agreed state of facts has been submitted, upon which he stands charged by the commonwealth with having obtained five thousand dollars from one Cornelius Rockham by false pretences. The facts are, briefly, that on the 17th day of December Barker called at the residence of Rockham and said that he desired to make a proposition looking to the recovery of the lost child of said Rockham, but he desired to make it in the presence of witnesses, and would return at ten o'clock that night. Pursuant to his appointment,

Barker again presented himself at the residence of said Rockham, and, in the presence of witnesses, declared, in substance, that at that time (then ten o'clock) he knew nothing of the said child, could not produce it, and could give no information in regard to it, but that at eleven o'clock he would know where the child was and would produce it; and that, if the said Rockham would then and there pay him five thousand dollars, he would at eleven o'clock take them to the lost child. The money was paid and the transaction completed.

"At eleven o'clock, Barker took the men to a certain corner in the upper part of this city, and it there developed that the entire matter was a scheme on his part for the purpose of obtaining the said sum of money, which he had in some manner disposed of; and that he in fact knew nothing of the child and never intended to produce it.

"The attorneys for the People considered it idle to discuss what they believed to be such a plain case of obtaining money under false pretences; and I confess that upon first hearing I was inclined to believe the proceeding a useless imposition upon the judiciary. I have had occasion to change my opinion."

The attorneys present looked at each other with wonder and drew their chairs closer to the table. The audience moved anxiously.

"The prisoner," continued the Judge, "has filed in his behalf the remarkable brief of one Randolph Mason, a counsellor. This I have read, first, with curiosity, then interest, then wonder, and, finally, conviction. In it the crime sought to be charged is traced from the days of the West Saxon Wights up to the present, beginning with the most ancient cases and ending with the later decisions of our own Court of Appeals. I have gone over these cases with great care, and find that the vital element of this crime is, and has ever been, the false and fraudulent representation or statement as to an *existing* or *past fact*. Hence, no representation, however false, in regard to a *future* transaction can be a crime. Nor can a false statement, *promissory* in its nature, be the subject of a criminal charge.

"To constitute this crime there must always be a false representation or statement as to a *fact*, and that *fact* must be a *past* or an *existing fact*. These are plain statements of ancient and well settled law, and laid here in this brief, almost in the exact language of our courts.

"In this case the vital element of crime is wanting. The evidence fails utterly to show false representation as to any *existing fact*. The prisoner, Barker, at the time of the transaction, positively disclaimed any knowledge of the child, or any ability to produce it. What he did represent was that he would know, and that he would perform certain things, in the future. The question of remoteness is irrelevant. It is immaterial whether the future time be removed minutes or years.

"The false representation complained of was wholly in regard to a future transaction, and essentially promissory in its nature, and such a wrong is not, and never has been, held to be the foundation of a criminal charge."

"But, if your Honor please," said the senior counsel for the People, rising, "is it not clearly evident that the prisoner, Barker, began with a design to defraud; that that design was present and obtained at the time of this transaction; that a representation was made to Rockham for the purpose of convincing him that there then existed a *bona fide* intention to produce his child; that money was obtained by false statements in regard to this intention then existing, when in fact such intention did not exist and never existed, and statements made to induce Rockham to believe that it did exist were all utterly false, fraudulent, and delusive? Surely this is a crime."

The attorney sat down with the air of one who had propounded an unanswerable proposition. The Judge adjusted his eyeglasses and began to turn the pages of a report. "I read," he said, "from the syllabus of the case of The People of New York vs. John H. Blanchard. 'An indictment for false pretenses may not be founded upon an assertion of an existing intention, although it did not in fact exist. There must be a false representation as to an existing fact.'

"Your statement, sir, in regard to intention, in this case is true, but it is no element of crime."

"But, sir," interposed the counsel for the People, now fully awake to the fact that Barker was slipping from his grasp, "I ask to hold this man for conspiracy and as a violator of the Statute of Cheats."

"Sir," said the Judge, with some show of impatience, "I call your attention to Scott's case and the leading case of Ranney. In the former, the learned Court announces that if the false and fraudulent representations are not criminal there can be no conspiracy; and, in the latter, the Court says plainly that false pretences in former statutes, and gross fraud or cheat in the more recent acts, mean essentially the same thing.

"You must further well know that this man could not be indicted at common law for cheat, because no false token was used, and because in respect to the instrumentality by which it was accomplished it had no special reference to the public interest.

"This case is most remarkable in that it bears all the marks of a gross and detestable fraud, and in morals is a vicious and grievous wrong, but under our law it is no crime and the offender cannot be punished."

"I understand your Honor to hold," said the baffled attorney, jumping to his feet, "that this man is guilty of no crime; that the dastardly act which he confesses to have done constitutes no crime, and that he is to go out of this court-room freed from every description of liability or responsibility to any criminal tribunal; that the law is so defective and its arm so short that it cannot pluck forth the offender and punish him when by every instinct of morality he is a criminal. If this be true, what a limitless field is open to the knave, and what a snug harbor for him is the great commonwealth of New York!"

"I can pardon your abruptness," said the Judge, looking down upon the angry and excited counsellor, "for the reason that your words are almost exactly the lament of presiding Justice Mullin in the case of Scott. But, sir, this is not a matter of sentiment; it is not a matter of morality; it is not even a matter of right. It is purely and simply a matter of law, and there is no law."

The Judge unconsciously arose and stood upright beside the bench. The audience of criminals bent forward in their seats.

"I feel," he continued, "for the first time the utter inability of the law to cope with the gigantic cunning of Evil. I appreciate the utter villainy that pervaded this entire transaction. I am convinced that it was planned with painstaking care by some master mind moved by Satanic impulse. I now know that there is abroad in this city a malicious intelligence of almost infinite genius, against which the machinery of the law is inoperative. Against every sentiment of common right, of common justice, I am compelled to decide that Lemuel Barker is guilty of no crime and stands acquit."

It was high noon. The audience of criminals passed out from the temple of so-called Justice, and with them went Lemuel Barker, unwhipped and brazen; now with ample means by which to wrest his fellows in villainy from the righteous wrath of the commonwealth. They were all enemies of this same commonwealth, bitter, never wearying enemies, and to-day they had learned much. How short-armed the Law was! Wondrous marvel that they had not known it sooner! To be sure they must plan so cunningly that only the Judge should pass upon them. He was a mere legal machine.

He was only the hand applying the rigid rule of the law. The danger was with the jury; there lay the peril to be avoided. The jury! how they hated it and feared it! and of right, for none knew better than they that whenever, and where-ever, and however men stop to probe for it, they always find, far down in the human heart, a great love of common right and fair dealing that is as deep-seated and abiding as the very springs of life.

VI—THE SHERIFF OF GULLMORE

[The crime of embezzlement here dealt with is statutory. The venue of this story could have been laid in many other States; the statutes are similar to a degree. See the Code of West Virginia; also the late case of The State vs. Bolin, 19 Southwestern Reporter, 650; also the long list of ancient cases in Russell on Crimes, 2d volume.]

I.

IT is hard luck, Colonel," said the broker, "but you are are not the only one skinned in the deal; the best of them caught it to-day. By Jupiter! the pit was like Dante's Inferno!"

"Yes, it's gone, I reckon," muttered the Colonel, shutting his teeth down tight on his cigar; "I guess the devil wins every two out of three."

"Well," said the broker, turning to his desk, "it is the fortune of war."

"No, young man," growled the Colonel, "it is the blasted misfortune of peace. I have never had any trouble with the fortune of war. I could stand on an ace high and win with war. It is peace that queers me. Here in the fag-end of the nineteenth century, I, Colonel Moseby Allen, sheriff of Gull-more County, West Virginia, go up against another man's game,—yes, and go up in the daytime. Say, young man, it feels queer at the mellow age of forty-nine, after you have been in the legislature of a great commonwealth, and at the very expiration of your term as sheriff of the whitest and the freest county in West Virginia,—I say it feels queer, after all those high honors, to be suddenly reminded that you need to be accompanied by a business chaperon."

The Colonel stood perfectly erect and delivered his oration with the fluency and the abandon of a southern orator. When he had finished, he bowed low to the broker, pulled his big slouch hat down on his forehead, and stalked out of the office and down the steps to the street.

Colonel Moseby Allen was built on the decided lines of a southern mountaineer. He was big and broad-shouldered, but he was not well proportioned. His body was short and heavy, while his legs were long. His eyes were deep-set and shone like little brown beads. On the whole, his face indicated cunning, bluster, and rashness. The ward politician would have recognized him among a thousand as a kindred spirit, and the professional gambler would not have felt so sure of himself with such a face across the table from him.

When the Colonel stepped out on the pavement, he stopped, thrust his hands into his pockets, and looked up and down Wall Street; then he jerked the cigar out of his mouth, threw it into the gutter, and began to deliver himself of a philippic upon the negative merits of brokers in general, and his broker in particular. The Virginian possessed a vocabulary of smooth billingsgate that in vividness and diversity approached the sublime. When he had consigned some seven generations of his broker's ancestry to divers minutely described localities in perdition, he began to warm to his work, and his artistic profanity rolled forth in startling periods.

The passers-by stopped and looked on in surprise and wonder. For a moment they were half convinced that the man was a religious fanatic, his eloquent, almost poetic, tirade was so thoroughly filled with holy names. The effect of the growing audience inspired the speaker. He raised his voice and began to emphasize with sweeping gestures. He had now finished with the broker's ancestry and was plunging with a rush of gorgeous pyrotechnics into the certain future of the broker himself, when a police officer pushed through the crowd and caught the irate Virginian by the shoulder.

Colonel Allen paused and looked down at the officer.

"You," he said, calmly, "I opine are a minion of the law; a hireling of the municipal authorities."

"See here," said the officer, "you are not allowed to preach on the street. You will have to come with me to the station-house."

The Colonel bowed suavely. "Sir," he said, "I, Colonel Moseby Allen, sheriff of Gullmore County in the Mountain State of West Virginia, am a respecter of the law, even in the body of its petty henchmen, and if the ordinances of this Godforsaken Gomorrah are such that a free-born American citizen, twenty-one years old and white, is not permitted the inalienable privilege of expressing his opinion without let or hindrance, then I am quite content to accompany you to the confines of your accursed jail-house."

Allen turned round and started down the street with the officer. He walked a little in advance, and continued to curse glibly in a low monotone. When they were half way to the corner below, a little man slipped out of the crowd and hurried up to the policeman. "Mike," he whispered, putting his hand under the officer's, "here is five for you. Turn him over to me."

The officer closed his hand like a trap, stepped quickly forward, and touched his prisoner on the shoulder.

As the Virginian turned, the officer said in a loud voice: "Mr. Parks, here, says that he knows you, and that you are all right, so I 'll let you go this time." Then, before any reply could be made, he vanished around the corner.

Colonel Allen regarded his deliverer with the air of a world-worn cynic. "Well," he said, "one is rarely delivered from the spoiler by the hand of his friend, and I cannot now recall ever having had you for an enemy. May I inquire what motive prompts this gracious courtesy?"

"Don't speak so loud," said Parks, stepping up close to the man. "I happen to know something about your loss, Colonel Allen, and perhaps also a way to regain it. Will you come with me?"

The Virginian whistled softly. "Yes," he said.

II.

This is a fine hotel," observed Colonel Allen, beginning to mellow under the mystic spell of a five-course dinner and a quart of Cliquot. "Devilish fine hotel, Mr. Parks. All the divers moneys which I in my official capacity have collected in taxes from the fertile county of Gullmore, would scarcely pay for the rich embellishment of the barber shop of this magnificent edifice."

"Well, Colonel," said the bald Parks, with a sad smile, "that would depend upon the amount of the revenues of your county. I presume that they are large, and consequently the office of sheriff a good one."

"Yes, sir," answered the Virginian, "it is generally considered desirable from the standpoint of prominence. The climate of Gullmore is salubrious. Its pasture lands are fertile, and its citizens cultured and refined to a degree unusual even in the ancient and aristocratic counties of the Old Dominion. And, sir,"—here the Colonel drew himself up proudly, and thrust his hand into the breast of his coat,—"I am proud, sir, —proud to declare that from time to time the good citizens of Gullmore, by means of their suffrage, and with large and comfortable majorities, have proclaimed me their favorite son and competent official. Six years ago I was in the legislature at Charleston as the trusted representative of this grand old county of Gullmore; and four years ago, after the fiercest and most bitterly contested political conflict of all the history of the South, I was elected to that most important and honorable office of sheriff,—to the lasting glory of my public fame, and the great gratification of the commonwealth."

"That gratification is now four years old?" mused Parks.

Colonel Moseby Allen darted a swift, suspicious glance at his companion, but in a moment it was gone, and he had dropped back into his grandiloquent discourse. "Yes, sir, the banner county of West Virginia, deserting her ancient and sacred traditions, and forgetting for the time the imperishable precepts of her patriotic fathers, has gone over to affiliate with the ungodly. We were beaten, sir,—beaten in this last engagement,—horse, foot, and dragoons,—beaten by a set of carpet-baggers,—a set of unregenerate political tricksters of such diabolical cunning that nothing but the gates of hell could have prevailed against them. Now, sir, now,—and I say it mournfully, there is nothing left to us in the county of Gullmore, save only honor."

"Honor," sneered Parks, "an imaginary rope to hold fools with! It wont fill a hungry stomach, or satisfy a delinquent account." The little clerk spoke the latter part of his sentence slowly and deliberately.

Again the suspicious expression passed over the face of Colonel Allen, leaving traces of fear and anxiety in its wake. His eyes, naturally a little crossed, drew in toward his nose, and the muscles around his mouth grew hard. For a moment he was silent, looking down into his glass; then, with an effort, he went on: "Yes, the whole shooting-match is in the hands of the Philistines. From the members of the County Court up to the important and responsible position which I have filled for the last four years, and when my accounts are finally wound up, I——"

"Your accounts," murmured Parks, "when they are finally wound up, what then?"

Every trace of color vanished from the Virginian's face, his heavy jaws trembled, and he caught hold of the arms of the chair to steady himself.

Parks did not look up. He seemed deeply absorbed in studying the bottom of his glass. For a moment Colonel Moseby Allen had been caught off his guard, but it was only for a moment. He straightened up and underwent a complete transformation. Then, bending forward, he said, speaking low and distinctly: "Look here, my friend, you are the best guesser this side of hell. Now, if you can pick a winning horse we will divide the pool."

The two men were at a table in a corner of the Hoffman café, and, as it chanced, alone in the room. Parks glanced around quickly, then he leaned over and said: "That depends on just one thing, Colonel."

"Turn up the cards," growled the Virginian, shutting his teeth down tight on his lip.

"Well," said Parks, "you must promise to stick to your rôle to the end, if you commence with the play."

The southerner leaned back in his chair and stroked his chin thoughtfully. Finally he dropped his hand and looked up. "All right," he muttered; "I'll stand by the deal; throw out the cards."

Parks moved his chair nearer to the table and leaned over on his elbow. "Colonel," he said, "there is only one living man who can set up a successful counter-plot against fate, that is dead certain to win, and that man is here in New York to-day. He is a great lawyer, and besides being that, he is the greatest plotter since the days of Napoleon. Not one of his clients ever saw the inside of a prison. He can show men how to commit crimes in such a way that the law cannot touch them. No matter how desperate the position may be, he can always show the man who is in it a way by which he can get out. There is no case so hopeless that he cannot manage it. If money is needed, he can show you how to get it—a plain, practical way, by which you can get what you need and as much as you need. He has a great mind, but he is strangely queer and erratic, and must be approached with extreme care, and only in a certain way. This man," continued the little clerk, lowering his voice, "is named Randolph Mason. You must go to him and explain the whole matter, and you must do it just in the way I tell you."

Again the Virginian whistled softly. "My friend," he said, "there is a little too much mystery about this matter. I am not afraid of you, because you are a rascal; no one ever had a face like you that was not a rascal. You will stick to me because you are out for the stuff, and there is no possible way to make a dollar by throwing the game. I am not afraid of any living man, if I have an opportunity to see his face before the bluff is made. You are all right; your game is to use me in making some haul that is a little too high for yourself. That is what you have been working up to, and you are a smooth operator, my friend. A greenhorn would have concluded long ago that you were a detective, but I knew a blamed sight better than that the moment you made your first lead. In the first place, you are too sharp to waste your time with any such bosh, and in the second place, it takes cash to buy detectives, and there is nobody following me with cash. Gullmore county has no kick coming to it until my final settlements are made, and there is no man treading shoe leather that knows anything about the condition of my official business except myself, and perhaps also that shrewd and mysterious guesser—yourself. So, you see, I am not standing on ceremonies with you. But here, young man, comes in a dark horse, and you want me to bet on him blindfolded. Those are not the methods of Moseby Allen. I must be let in a little deeper on this thing."

"All I want you to do," said Parks, putting his hand confidentially on the Virginian's arm, "is simply to go and see Randolph Mason, and approach him in the way I tell you, and when you have done that, I will wager that you stay and explain everything to him."

Colonel Allen leaned back in his chair and thrust his hands into his pockets. "Why should I do that?" he said curtly.

"Well," murmured the little man mournfully, "one's bondsmen are entitled to some consideration; and then, there is the penitentiary. Courts have a way of sending men there for embezzlement."

"You are correct," said Allen, quietly, "and I have not time to go."

"At any rate," continued Parks, "there can be no possible danger to you. You are taking no chances. Mr. Mason is a member of the New York bar, and anything you may tell him he dare not reveal. The law would not permit him to do so if he desired. The whole matter would be kept as thoroughly inviolate as though it were made in the confessional. Your objections are all idle. You are a man in a desperate position. You are up to your waist in the quicksand, now, and, at the end of the year, it is bound to close over your head. It is folly to look up at the sky and attempt to ignore this fact. I offer to help you—not from any goodness of heart, understand, but because we can both make a stake in this thing. I need money, and you must have money,—that is the whole thing in a nutshell. Now," said Parks, rising from his chair, "what are you going to do?"

"Well," said the Virginian, drawing up his long legs and spreading out his fat hands on the table, "*Colonel Moseby Allen, of the county of Gullmore, will take five cards, if you please.*"

III.

This must be the place," muttered the Virginian, stopping under the electric light and looking up at the big house on the avenue. "That fellow said I would know the place by the copper-studded door, and there it is, as certain as there are back taxes in Gullmore." With that, Colonel Moseby Allen walked up the granite steps and began to grope about in the dark door-way for the electric bell. He could find no trace of this indispensable convenience, and was beginning to lapse into a flow of half-suppressed curses, when he noticed for the first time an ancient silver knocker fastened to the middle of the door. He seized it and banged it vigorously.

The Virginian stood in the dark and waited. Finally he concluded that the noise had not been heard, and was about to repeat the signal when the door was flung suddenly open, and a tall man holding a candle in his hand loomed up in the door-way.

"I am looking," stammered the southerner, "for one Randolph Mason, an attorney-at-law."

"I am Randolph Mason," said the man, thrusting the silver candlestick out before him. "Who are you, sir?"

"My name is Allen," answered the southerner, "Moseby Allen, of

Gullmore county, West Virginia."

"A Virginian," said Mason, "what evil circumstance brings you here?"

Then Allen remembered the instructions which Parks had given him so minutely. He took off his hat and passed his hand across his forehead. "Well," he said, "I suppose the same thing that brings the others. We get in and plunge along just as far as we can. Then Fate shuts down the lid of her trap, and we have either to drop off the bridge or come here."

"Come in," said Mason. Then he turned abruptly and walked down the hall-way. The southerner followed, impressed by this man's individuality. Allen had pushed his way through life with bluff and bluster, and like that one in the scriptural writings, "neither feared God nor regarded man." His unlimited assurance had never failed him before any of high or low degree, and to be impressed with the power of any man was to him strange and uncomfortable.

Mason turned into his library and placed the candlestick on a table in the centre of the floor. Then he drew up two chairs and sat down in one of them motioning Allen to the other on the opposite side of the table. The room was long and empty, except for the rows of heavy book-cases standing back in the darkness. The floor was bare, and there was no furniture of any kind whatever, except the great table and the ancient high-back chairs. There was no light but the candle standing high in its silver candlestick.

"Sir," said Mason, when the Virginian had seated himself, "which do you seek to evade, punishment or dishonor?"

The Virginian turned round, put his elbows on the table, and looked squarely across at his questioner. "I am not fool enough to care for the bark," he answered, "provided the dog's teeth are muzzled."

"It is well," said Mason, slowly, "there is often difficulty in dealing with double problems, where both disgrace and punishment are sought to be evaded. Where there is but one difficulty to face, it can usually be handled with ease. What others are involved in your matter?"

"No others," answered the Virginian; "I am seeking only to save myself."

"From the law only," continued Mason, "or does private vengeance join with it?"

"From the law only," answered Allen.

"Let me hear it all," said Mason.

"Well," said the Virginian, shifting uneasily in his chair, "my affairs are in a very bad way, and every attempt that I have made to remedy them has resulted only in disaster. I am walking, with my hands tied, straight into the penitentiary, unless some miracle can be performed in my favor. Everything has gone dead against me from my first fool move. Four years ago I was elected sheriff of Gullmore county in the State of West Virginia. I was of course required by law to give a large bond. This I had much difficulty in doing, for the reason that I have no estate whatever. Finally I induced my brother and my father, who is a very old man, to mortgage their property and thereby secured the requisite bond. I entered upon the duties of my office, and assumed entire control of the revenues of the county. For a time I managed them carefully and kept my private business apart from that of the county. But I had never been accustomed to strict business methods, and I soon found it most difficult to confine myself to them. Little by little I began to lapse into my old habit of carelessness. I neglected to keep up the settlements, and permitted the official business to become intermixed with my private accounts. The result was that I awoke one morning to find that I owed the county of Gullmore ten thousand dollars. I began at once to calculate the possibility of my being able to meet this deficit before the expiration of my term of office, and soon found that by no possible means would I be able to raise this amount out of the remaining fees. My gambling instincts at once asserted themselves. I took five thousand dollars, went to Lexington, and began to play the races in a vain, reckless hope that I might win enough to square my accounts. I lost from the very start. I came back to my county and went on as before, hoping against hope that something would turn up and let me out. Of course this was the dream of an idiot, and when the opposition won at the last election, and a new sheriff was installed, and I was left but a few months within which to close up my accounts, the end which I had refused to think of arose and stared me in the face. I was now at the end of my tether, and there was nothing there but a tomb. And even that way was not open. If I should escape the penitentiary by flight or by suicide, I would still leave my brother and my aged father to bear the entire burden of my defalcations; and when they, as my bondsmen, had paid the sum to the county, they would all be paupers."

The man paused and mopped the perspiration from his face. He was now terribly in earnest, and seemed to be realizing the gravity and the hopelessness of his crime. All his bluster and grandiloquent airs had vanished.

"Reckless and unscrupulous as I am," he went on, "I cannot bear to think of my brother's family beggars because of my wrong, or my father in his extreme old age turned out from under his own roof and driven into the poor-house, and yet it must come as certainly as the sun will rise tomorrow."

The man's voice trembled now, and the flabby muscles of his face quivered.

"In despair, I gathered up all the funds of the county remaining in my hands and hurried to this city. Here I went to the most reliable broker I could find and through him plunged into speculation. But all the devils in hell seemed to be fighting for my ruin. I was caught in that dread and unexpected crash of yesterday and lost everything. Strange to say, when I realized that my ruin was now complete, I felt a kind of exhilaration,— such, I presume, as is said to come to men when they are about to be executed. Standing in the very gaping jaws of ruin, I have to-day been facetious, even merry. Now, in the full glare of this horrible matter, I scarcely remember what I have been doing, or how I came to be here, except that this morning in Wall Street I heard some one speak of your ability, and I hunted up your address and came without any well defined plan, and, if you will pardon me, I will add that it was also without any hope."

The man stopped and seemed to settle back in his chair in a great heap.

Randolph Mason arose and stood looking down at the Virginian.

"Sir," said Mason, "none are ever utterly lost but the weak. Answer my question."

The Virginian pulled himself together and looked up.

"Is there any large fund," continued Mason, "in the hands of the officers of your county?"

"My successor," said Allen, "has just collected the amount of a levy ordered by the county court for the purpose of paying the remainder due on the court-house. He now has that fund in his hands."

"When was the building erected?" said Mason.

"It was built during the last year of my term of office, and paid for in part out of levies ordered while I was active sheriff. When my successor came in there still remained due the contractors on the work some thirty thousand dollars. A levy was ordered by the court shortly before my term expired, but the collection of this levy fell to the coming officer, so this money is not in my hands, although all the business up to this time has been managed by me, and the other payments on the building made from time to time out of moneys in my hands, and I have been the chief manager of the entire work and know more about it than any one else. The new sheriff came into my office a few days ago to inquire how he was to dispose of this money."

Mason sat down abruptly. "Sir," he said almost bitterly, "there is not enough difficulty in your matter to bother the cheapest intriguer in Kings county. I had hoped that yours was a problem of some gravity."

"I see," said the Virginian, sarcastically, "I am to rob the sheriff of this money in such a manner that it won't be known who received it, and square my accounts. That would be very easy indeed. I would have only to kill three men and break a bank. Yes, that would be very easy. You might as well tell me to have blue eyes."

"Sir," said Randolph Mason, slowly, "you are the worst prophet unhung."

"Well," continued the man, "there can be no other way, If it were turned over to me in my official capacity what good would it do? My bondsmen would be responsible for it. I would then have it to account for, and what difference, in God's name, can it make whether I am sent to the penitentiary for stealing money which I have already used, or for stealing this money? It all belongs to the county. It is two times six one way, and six times two the other way."

"Sir," said Mason, "I retract my former statement in regard to your strong point. Let me insist that you devote your time to prophecy. Your reasoning is atrocious."

"I am wasting my time here," muttered the Virginian, "there is no way out of it."

Randolph Mason turned upon the man. "Are you afraid of courts?" he growled.

"No," said the southerner, "I am afraid of nothing but the penitentiary."

"Then," said Mason, leaning over on the table, "listen to me, and you will never see the shadow of it."

IV.

Isuppose you are right about that," said Jacob Wade, the newly elected sheriff of Gullmore county, as he and Colonel Moseby Allen sat in the office of that shrewd and courteous official. "I suppose it makes no

difference which one of us takes this money and pays the contractors,—
we are both under good bonds, you know."

"Certainly, Wade, certainly," put in the Colonel, "your bond is as good as
they can be made in Gullmore county, and I mean no disrespect to the
Omnipotent Ruler of the Universe when I assert that the whole kingdom
of heaven could not give a better bond than I have. You are right, Wade;
you are always right; you are away ahead of the ringleaders of your
party. I don't mind if I do say so. Of course, I am on the other side, but it
was miraculous, I tell you, the way you swung your forces into line in the
last election. By all the limping gods of the calendar, we could not touch
you!" Colonel Moseby Allen leaned over and patted his companion on
the shoulder. "You are a sly dog, Wade," he continued. "If it had not
been for you we would have beaten the bluebells of Scotland out of the
soft-headed farmers who were trying to run your party. I told the boys
you would pull the whole ticket over with you, but they did n't believe
me. Next time they will have more regard for the opinion of Moseby
Allen of Gull-more." The Colonel burst out into a great roar of laughter,
and brought his fat hand down heavily on his knee.

Jacob Wade, the new sheriff, was a cadaverous-looking countryman,
with a face that indicated honesty and egotism. He had come up from a
farm, and had but little knowledge of business methods in general, and
no idea of how the duties of his office should be properly performed. He
puffed up visibly under the bald flattery of Allen, and took it all in like a
sponge.

"Well," said Wade, "I suppose the boys did sort of expect me to help
them over, and I guess I did. I have been getting ready to run for a long
time, and I aint been doing no fool things. When the Farmers Alliance
people was organizing, I just stayed close home and sawed wood, and
when the county was all stirred up about that there dog tax, I kept my
mouth shut, and never said nothing."

"That 's what you did, Wade," continued the Colonel, rubbing his hands;
"you are too smooth to get yourself mixed up with a lot of new-fangled
notions that would brand you all over the whole county as a crank. What
a man wants in order to run for the office of sheriff is a reputation for

being a square, solid, substantial business man, and that is what you had, Wade, and besides that you were a smooth, shrewd, far-sighted, machine politician."

Jacob Wade flushed and grew pompous under this eloquent recital of his alleged virtues. Allen was handling his man with skill. He was a natural judge of men, and possessed in no little degree the rare ability of knowing how to approach the individual in order to gain his confidence and goodwill.

"No," he went on, "I am not partisan enough to prevent me from appreciating a good clearheaded politician, no matter what his party affiliations may be. I am as firm and true to my principles as any of those high up in the affairs of state. I have been honored by my party time and again in the history of this commonwealth, and have defended and supported her policies on the stump, and in the halls of legislation, and I know a smooth man when I see him, and I honor him, and stick to him out of pure love for his intelligence and genius."

The Colonel arose. He now felt that his man was in the proper humor to give ready assent to the proposition which he had made, and he turned back to it with careless indifference.

"Now, Jacob," he said lowering his voice, "this is not all talk. You are a new officer, and I am an old one. I am familiar with all the routine business of the sheriffalty, and I am ready and willing and anxious to give all the information that can be of any benefit to you, and to do any and everything in my power to make your term of office as pleasant and profitable as it can be made. I am wholly and utterly at your service, and want you to feel that you are more than welcome to command me in any manner you see fit. By the way, here is this matter that we were just discussing. I am perfectly familiar with all that business. I looked after the building for the county, collected all the previous levies, and know all about the contracts with the builders—just what is due each one and just how the settlements are to be made,—and I am willing to take charge of this fund and settle the thing up. I suppose legally it is my duty to attend to this work, as it is in the nature of unfinished business of my term, but I could have shifted the whole thing over on you and gotten out of the trouble of making the final settlements with the contractors. The levy was ordered during my term, but has been collected by you, and on that ground I could have washed my hands of the troublesome matter if I had been disposed to be ugly. But I am not that kind of a man, Wade; I am willing to shoulder my lawful duties, and wind this thing up and leave your office clear and free from any old matters."

Jacob Wade, sheriff of Gullmore county, was now thoroughly convinced of two things. First, that he himself was a shrewd politician, with an intellect of almost colossal proportions, and second, that Colonel Moseby Allen was a great and good man, who was offering to do him a service out of sheer kindness of heart.

He arose and seized Allen's hand. "I am obliged to you, Colonel, greatly obliged to you," he said; "I don't know much about these matters yet, and it will save me a deal of trouble if you will allow me to turn this thing over to you, and let you settle it up. I reckon from the standpoint of law it is a part of your old business as sheriff."

"Yes," answered Allen, smiling broadly, "I reckon it is, and I reckon I ought n't to shirk it."

"All right," said Wade, turning to leave the office, "I 'll just hand the whole thing over to you in the morning." Then he went out.

The ex-sheriff closed the door, sat down in his chair, and put his feet on the table. "Well, Moseby, my boy," he said, "that was dead easy. The Honorable Jacob Wade is certainly the most irresponsible idiot west of the Alleghany mountains. He ought to have a committee,—yes, he ought to have two committees, one to run him, and one to run his business." Then he rubbed his hands gleefully. "It is working like a greased clock," he chuckled, "and by the grace of God and the Continental Congress, when this funeral procession does finally start, it wont be Colonel Moseby Allen of the county of Gullmore who will occupy the hearse."

V.

The inhabitants of the city could never imagine the vast interest aroused in the county of Gullmore by the trial of Colonel Moseby Allen for embezzlement. In all their quiet lives the good citizens had not been treated to such a sweeping tidal wave of excitement. The annual visits of the "greatest show on earth" were scarcely able to fan the interests of the countrymen into such a flame. The news of Allen's arrest had spread through the country like wildfire. Men had talked of nothing else from the moment this startling information had come to their ears. The crowds on Saturday afternoons at the country store had constituted themselves courts of first and last resort, and had passed on the matter of the ex-sheriff's guilt at great length and with great show of learning. The village blacksmith had delivered ponderous opinions while he shod the traveller's horse; and the ubiquitous justice of the peace had demonstrated time and again with huge solemnity that Moseby Allen was a great criminal, and by no possible means could be saved from conviction. It was the general belief that the ex-sheriff would not stand trial; that he would by some means escape from the jail where he was confined. So firm-rooted had this conviction become that the great crowd gathered in the little county seat on the day fixed for the trial were considerably astonished when they saw the ex-sheriff sitting in the dock. In the evening after the first day of the trial, in which certain wholly unexpected things had come to pass, the crowd gathered on the porch of the country hotel were fairly revelling in the huge sensation.

Duncan Hatfield, a long ungainly mountaineer, wearing a red hunting-shirt and a pair of blue jeans trousers, was evidently the Sir-Oracle of the occasion.

"I tell you, boys," he was saying, "old Moseby aint got no more show than a calliker apron in a brush fire. Why he jest laid down and give up; jest naturally lopped his ears and give up like a whipped dog."

"Yes," put in an old farmer who was standing a little back in the crowd, "I reckon nobody calkerlated on jest sich a fizzle."

"When he come into court this mornin'," continued the Oracle, "with that there young lawyer man Edwards, I poked Lum Bozier in the side, and told him to keep his eye skinned, and he would see the fur fly, because I knowed that Sam Lynch, the prosecutin' attorney, allowed to go fer old Moseby, and Sam is a fire-eater, so he is, and he aint afraid of nuthin that walks on legs. But, Jerusalem! it war the tamest show that ever come to this yer town. Edwards jest sot down and lopped over like a weed, and Sam he begun, and he showed up how old Moseby had planned this here thing, and how he had lied to Jake Wade all the way through, and jest how he got that there money, and what an everlasting old rascal he was, and there sot Edwards, and he never asked no questions, and he never paid no attention to nuthin."

"Did n't the lawyer feller do nuthin at all, Dunk?" enquired one of the audience, who had evidently suffered the great misfortune of being absent from the trial.

"No," answered the Oracle, with a bovine sneer, "he never did nothin till late this evenin. Then he untangled his legs and got up and said somethin to the jedge about havin to let old Moseby Allen go, cause what he had done was n't no crime.

"Then you ought to a heard Sam. He jest naturally took the roof off; he sailed into old Moseby. He called him nine different kinds of horse-thieves, and when he got through, I could see old Ampe Props noddin his head back thar in the jury-box, and then I knowed that it were all up with Colonel Moseby Allen, cause that jury will go the way old Ampe goes, jest like a pack of sheep."

"I reckon Moseby's lawyer were skeered out," suggested Pooley Hornick, the blacksmith.

"I reckon he war," continued the Oracle, "cause when Sam sot down, he got up, and he said to the jedge that he didn't want to do no argufying, but he had a little paper that would show why the jedge would have to let old Moseby go free, and then he asked Sam if he wanted to see it, and Sam he said no, he cared nuthin for his little paper. Then the feller went over and give the little paper to the jedge, and the jedge he took it and he said he would decide in the mornin'."

"You don't reckon," said the farmer, "that the jedge will give the old colonel any show, do you?"

"Billdad Solsberry," said the Oracle, with a grave judicial air, as though to settle the matter beyond question, "you are a plumb fool. If the angel Gabriel war to drop down into Gullmore county, he could n't keep old Moseby Allen from goin' to the penitentiary."

Thus the good citizens sat in judgment, and foretold the doom of their fellow.

VI.

On Monday night, the eleventh day of May, in the thirty-third year of the State of West Virginia, the judge of the criminal court of Gullmore county, and the judge of the circuit court of Gullmore county were to meet together for the purpose of deciding two matters,—one relating to the trial of Moseby Allen, the retiring sheriff, for embezzling funds of the county, amounting to thirty thousand dollars, and the other, an action pending in the circuit court, wherein the State of West Virginia, at the relation of Jacob Wade, was seeking to recover this sum from the bondsmen of Allen. In neither of the two cases was there any serious doubt as to the facts. It seemed that it was customary for the retiring sheriff to retain an office in the court building after the installation of his successor, and continue to attend to the unfinished business of the county until all his settlements had been made, and until all the matters relating to his term of office had been finally wound up and administered.

In accordance with this custom, Moseby Allen, after the expiration of his term, had continued in his office in a quasi-official capacity, in order to collect back taxes and settle up all matters carried over from his regular term.

It appeared that during Allen's term of office the county had built a court-house, and had ordered certain levies for the purpose of raising the necessary funds. The first of the levies had been collected by Allen, and paid over by him to the contractors, as directed by the county court. The remaining levies had not been collected during his term, but had been collected by the new sheriff immediately after his installation. This money, amounting to some thirty thousand dollars, had been turned over to Allen upon his claim that it grew out of the unfinished affairs of his term, and that, therefore, he was entitled to its custody. He had said to the new sheriff that the levy upon which it had been raised was ordered during his term, and the work for which it was to be paid all performed, and the bonds of the county issued, while he was active sheriff, and that he believed it was a part of the matters which were involved in his final settlements. Jacob Wade, then sheriff, believing that Allen was in fact the proper person to rightly administer this fund, and knowing that his bond to the county was good and would cover all his official affairs, had turned the entire fund over to him, and paid no further attention to the matter.

It appeared that, at the end of the year, Moseby Allen had made all of his proper and legitimate settlements fully and satisfactorily, and had accounted to the proper authorities for every dollar that had been collected by him during his term of office, but had refused and neglected to account for the money which he had received from Wade. When approached upon the subject, he had said plainly that he had used this money in unfortunate speculations and could not return it. The man had made no effort to check the storm of indignation that burst upon him; he firmly refused to discuss the matter, or to give any information in regard to it. When arrested, he had expressed no surprise, and had gone to the jail with the officer. At the trial, his attorney had simply waited until the evidence had been introduced, and had then arisen and moved the court to direct a verdict of not guilty, on the ground that Allen, upon the facts shown, had committed no crime punishable under the statutes of West Virginia.

The court had been strongly disposed to overrule this motion without stopping to consider it, but the attorney had insisted that a memorandum which he handed up would sustain his position, and that without mature consideration the judge ought not to force him into the superior court, whereupon his Honor, Ephraim Haines, had taken the matter under advisement until morning.

In the circuit court the question had been raised that Allen's bond covered only those matters which arose by virtue of his office, and that this fund was not properly included. Whereupon the careful judge of that court had adjourned to consider.

It was almost nine o'clock when the Honorable Ephraim Haines walked into the library to consult with his colleague of the civil court. He found that methodical jurist seated before a pile of reports, with his spectacles far out on the end of his nose,—an indication, as the said Haines well knew, that the said jurist had arrived at a decision, and was now carefully turning it over in his mind in order to be certain that it was in spirit and truth the very law of the land.

"Well, Judge," said Haines, "have you flipped the penny on it, and if so, who wins?"

The man addressed looked up from his book and removed his spectacles. He was an angular man, with a grave analytical face.

"It is not a question of who wins, Haines," he answered; "it is a question of law. I was fairly satisfied when the objection was first made, but I wanted to be certain before I rendered my decision. I have gone over the authorities, and there is no question about the matter. The bondsmen of Allen are not liable in this action."

"They are not!" said Haines, dropping his long body down into a chair. "It is public money, and the object of the bond is certainly to cover any defalcations."

"This bond," continued the circuit judge, "provides for the faithful discharge, according to law, of the duties of the office of sheriff during his continuance in said office. Moseby Allen ceased to be sheriff of this county the day his successor was installed, and on that day this bond ceased to cover his acts. This money was handed over by the lawful sheriff to a man who was not then an officer of this county. Moseby

Allen had no legal right to the custody of this money. His duties as sheriff had ceased, his official acts had all determined, and there was no possible way whereby he could then perform an official act that would render his bondsmen liable. The action pending must be dismissed. The present sheriff, Wade, is the one responsible to the county for this money. His only recourse is an action of debt, or assumpsit, against Allen individually, and as Allen is notoriously insolvent, Wade and his bondsmen will have to make up this deficit."

"Well," said Haines, "that is hard luck."

"No," answered the judge, "it is not luck at all, it is law. Wade permitted himself to be the dupe of a shrewd knave, and he must bear the consequences."

"You can depend upon it," said the Honorable Ephraim Haines, criminal judge by a political error, "that old Allen won't get off so easy with me. The jury will convict him, and I will land him for the full term."

"I was under the impression," said the circuit judge, gravely, "that a motion had been made in your court to direct an acquittal on the ground that no crime had been committed."

"It was," said Haines, "but of course it was made as a matter of form, and there is nothing in it."

"Have you considered it?"

"What is the use? It is a fool motion."

"Well," continued the judge, "this matter comes up from your court to mine on appeal, and you should be correct in your ruling. What authorities were cited?"

"Here is the memorandum," said the criminal judge, "you can run down the cases if you want to, but I know it is no use. The money belonged to the county and old Allen embezzled it,—that is admitted."

To this the circuit judge did not reply. He took the memorandum which Randolph Mason had prepared for Allen, and which the local attorney had submitted, and turned to the cases of reports behind him. He was a hard-working, conscientious man, and not least among his vexatious cares were the reckless decisions of the Honorable Ephraim Haines.

The learned judge of the criminal court put his feet on the table and began to whistle. When at length wearied of this intellectual diversion, he concentrated all the energy of his mammoth faculties on the highly cultured pastime of sharpening his penknife on the back of the Code.

At length the judge of the circuit court came back to the table, sat down, and adjusted his spectacles. "Haines," he said slowly, "you will have to sustain that motion."

"What!" cried the Honorable Ephraim, bringing the legs of his chair down on the floor with a bang.

"That motion," continued the judge, "must be sustained. Moseby Allen has committed no crime under the statutes of West Virginia."

"Committed no crime!" almost shouted the criminal jurist, doubling his long legs up under his chair, "why, old Allen admits that he got this money and spent it. He says that he converted it to his own use; that it was not his money; that it belonged to the county. The evidence of the State shows that he cunningly induced Wade to turn this money over to him, saying that his bond was good, and that he was entitled to the custody of the fund. The old rascal secured the possession of this money by trickery, and kept it, and now you say he has committed no crime. How in Satan's name do you figure it out?"

"Haines," said the judge, gravely, "I don't figure it out. The law cannot be figured out. It is certain and exact. It describes perfectly what wrongs are punishable as crimes, and exactly what elements must enter into each wrong in order to make it a crime. All right of discretion is taken from the trial court; the judge must abide by the law, and the law decides matters of this nature in no uncertain terms."

"Surely," interrupted Haines, beginning to appreciate the gravity of the situation, "old Allen can be sent to the penitentiary for this crime. He is a rank, out and out embezzler. He stole this money and converted it to his own use. Are you going to say that the crime of embezzlement is a dead letter?"

"My friend," said the judge, "you forget that there is no equity in the criminal courts. The crime of embezzlement is a pure creature of the statute. Under the old common law there was no such crime. Consequently society had no protection from wrongs of this nature, until this evil grew to such proportions that the law-making power began by statute to define this crime and provide for its punishment. The ancient English statutes were many and varied, and, following in some degree thereafter, each of the United States has its own particular statute, describing this crime as being composed of certain fixed technical elements. This indictment against Moseby Allen is brought under Section 19 of Chapter 145 of the Code of West Virginia, which provides: 'If any officer, agent, clerk or servant of this State, or of any county, district, school district or municipal corporation thereof, or of any incorporated bank or other corporation, or any officer of public trust in this State, or any agent, clerk or servant of such officer of public trust, or any agent, clerk or servant of any firm or person, or company or association of persons not incorporated, embezzle or fraudulently convert to his own use, bullion, money, bank notes or other security for money, or any effects or property of another person which shall have come to his possession, or been placed under his care or management, by virtue of his office, place or employment, he shall be guilty of larceny thereof.'

"This is the statute describing the offence sought to be charged. All such statutes must be strictly construed. Applying these requisites of the crime to the case before us, we find that Allen cannot be convicted, for the reason that at the time this money was placed in his hands he was not sheriff of Gullmore county, nor was he in any sense its agent, clerk, or servant. And, second, if he could be said to continue an agent, clerk, or servant of this county, after the expiration of his term, he would continue such agent, clerk, or servant for the purpose only of administering those matters which might be said to lawfully pertain to the unfinished business of his office. This fund was in no wise connected with such unfinished affairs, and by no possible construction could he be said to be an agent, clerk, or servant of this county for the purpose of its distribution or custody. Again, in order to constitute such embezzlement, the money must have come into his possession by virtue of his office. This could not be, for the reason that he held no office. His time, had expired; Jacob Wade was sheriff, and the moment Jacob Wade was installed, Allen's official capacity determined, and he became a private citizen, with only the rights and liabilities of such a citizen.

"Nor is he guilty of larceny, for the very evident reason that the proper custodian, Wade, voluntarily placed this money in his hands, and he received it under a *bona fide* color of right."

The Honorable Ephraim Haines arose, and brought his ponderous fist down violently on the table. "By the Eternal!" he said, "this is the cutest trick that has been played in the two Virginias for a century. Moseby Allen has slipped out of the clutches of the law like an eel."

"Ephraim," said the circuit judge, reproachfully, "this is no frivolous matter. Moseby Allen has wrought a great wrong, by which many innocent men will suffer vast injury, perhaps ruin. Such malicious cunning is dangerous to society. Justice cannot reach all wrongs; its hands are tied by the restrictions of the law. Why, under this very statute, one who was *de facto* an officer of the county or State, by inducing some other officer to place in his hands funds to which he was not legally entitled, could appropriate the funds so received with perfect impunity, and without committing any crime or rendering his bondsmen liable. Thus a clerk of the circuit court could use without criminal liability any money, properly belonging to the clerk of the county court, or sheriff, provided he could convince the clerk or sheriff that he was entitled to its custody; and so with any officer of the State or county, and this could be done with perfect ease where the officers were well known to each other and strict business methods were not observed. Hence all the great wrong and injury of embezzlement can be committed, and all the gain and profit of it be secured, without violating the statute or rendering the officer liable to criminal prosecution. It would seem that the rogue must be stupid indeed who could not evade the crime of embezzlement."

The man stopped, removed his spectacles, and closed them up in their case. He was a painstaking, honest servant of the commonwealth, and, like many others of the uncomplaining strong, performed his own duties and those of his careless companion without murmur or comment or hope of reward.

The Honorable Ephraim Haines arose and drew himself up pompously. "I am glad," he said, "that we agree on this matter. I shall sustain this motion."

The circuit judge smiled grimly. "Yes," he said, "it is not reason or justice, but it is the law."

At twelve the following night Colonel Moseby Allen, ex-sheriff of the county of Gullmore, now acquitted of crime by the commonwealth, hurried across the border for the purpose of avoiding certain lawless demonstrations on the part of his countrymen,—and of all his acts of public service, this was the greatest.

VII.—THE ANIMUS FURANDI

[See the case of State vs. Brown et al.% 104 Mo., 365; the strange case of Reuben Deal, 64 N. C., 270; also on all fours with the facts here involved, see Thompson vs. Commonwealth, 18 S. W. Rept., 3022; and the very recent case of The People vs. Hughes, 39 Pacific Rept., 492; also Rex vs. Hall, Bodens case, and others there cited, 2 Russell on Crimes.]

I.

IAM tired of your devilish hints, why can't you come out with it, man?" The speaker was half angry.

Parks leaned forward on the table, his face was narrow and full of cunning. "Mystery is your long suit, Hogarth, I compliment you."

"You tire me," said the man; "if you have any reason for bringing me here at this hour of the night I want to know it."

"Would I be here in the office at two o'clock in the morning, with a detective and without a reason? Listen, I will be plain with you. I must get Mr. Mason out of New York; he is going rapidly, and unless he gets a sea-voyage and a change of country he will be in the mad-house. He is terribly thin and scarcely sleeps any more at all. No human being can imagine what a monster he is to manage, or in what an infinitely difficult position I have been placed. When we came here from Paris, after the unfortunate collapse of the canal syndicate, the situation that confronted me was of the most desperate character. Mr. Mason was practically a bankrupt. He had spent his entire fortune in a mighty effort to right the syndicate, and would have succeeded if it had not been for the treachery of some of the French officials. He had been absent so long from New York that his law practice was now entirely lost, and, worst of all, this mysterious tilt of his mind would render it utterly impossible for him ever to regain his clientage. For a time I was in despair. Mr. Mason was, of course, utterly oblivious to the situation, and there was no one with whom I could advise, even if I dared attempt it. When everything failed in Paris, Mr. Mason collapsed, physically. He was in the hospital for months; when he came out, his whole nature was wrenched into this strange groove, although his mind was apparently as keen and powerful as ever and his wonderful faculties unimpaired. He seemed now possessed by this one idea, that all the difficulties of men were problems and that he could solve them.

"A few days after we landed in New York, I wandered into the court-house; a great criminal had been apprehended and was being tried for a desperate crime. I sat down and listened. As the case developed, it occurred to me that the man had botched his work fearfully, and that if he could have had Mr. Mason plan his crime for him he need never have been punished. Then the inspiration came. Why not turn this idea of Mr. Mason to account?

"I knew that the city was filled with shrewd, desperate men, who feared nothing under high heaven but the law, and were willing to take desperate chances with it. I went to some of them and pointed out the mighty aid that I could give; they hooted at the idea, and said that crime was crime and the old ways were the best ways."

Parks paused and looked up at the detective. "They have since changed their minds," he added.

"What did Mr. Mason think of your method of securing clients?" said Hogarth.

"That was my greatest difficulty," continued Parks. "I resorted to every known trick in order to prevent him from learning how the men happened to come to him, and so far I have been successful. He has never suspected me, and has steadily believed that those who came to him with difficulties were attracted by his great reputation. By this means, Mr. Mason has made vast sums of money, but what he has done with it is a mystery. I have attempted to save what I could, but I have not enough for this extended trip to the south of France. Now, do you understand me?"

"Yes," answered the detective, "you want to find where his money is hidden."

"No," said Parks, with a queer smile, "I am not seeking impossible ventures. What Randolph Mason chooses to make a mystery will remain so to the end of time, all the detectives on the earth to the contrary."

"What do you want, then?" asked Hogarth, doggedly.

Parks drew his chair nearer to the man and lowered his voice. "My friend," he said, "this recent change in the administration of the city has thrown you out on your uppers. Your chief is gone for good, and with him all your hopes in New York. It was a rout, my friend, and they have all saved themselves but you. What is to become of you?"

"God knows!" said the detective. "Of course I am still a member of the agency, but there is scarcely bread in that."

"This world is a fighting station," continued Parks. "The one intention of the entire business world is robbery. The man on the street has no sense of pity; he grows rich because he conceives some shrewd scheme by which he is enabled to seize and enjoy the labor of others. His only object is to avoid the law; he commits the same wrong and causes the same resulting injury as the pirate. The word 'crime,' Hogarth, was invented by the strong with which to frighten the weak; it means nothing. Now listen, since the thing is a cutthroat game, why not have our share of the spoil?" Hogarth's face was a study; Parks was shrewdly forcing the right door.

"My friend," the little man went on, "we can make a fortune by a twist of the wrist, and go scot-free with the double eagles clinking in our pockets. We can make it in a day, and thereafter wag our heads at fortune and snap our fingers at the law."

"How?" asked the detective. The door had broken and swung in.

"I will tell you," said Parks, placing his hand confidentially on the man's shoulder. "Mr. Mason has a plan. I know it, because yesterday he was walking up Broadway, apparently oblivious to everything. Suddenly his face cleared up, and he stopped and snapped his fingers. 'Good!' he said, 'a detective could do it, and it would be child play, child play.'"

Hogarth's countenance fell. "Is that all?" he said.

"All!" echoed Parks, bringing his hand down on the table. "Is n't that enough, man? You don't know Randolph Mason. If he has a plan by which a detective can make a haul, it is good, do you hear, and it goes."

"What does this mean, Parks?" said a voice.

The little clerk sprang up and whirled round. In his vehemence he had not noticed the door-way. Randolph Mason stood in the shadow. He was thin and haggard, his face was shrunken and unshaven, and he looked worn and exhausted.

"Oh, sir," said Parks, gathering himself quickly, "this is my friend Braxton Hogarth, and he is in great trouble. He came here to ask me for help; we have been talking over the matter for many hours, and I don't see any way out for him."

"Where has the trap caught him?" said Mason, coming into the room.

"It is an awful strange thing, sir," answered the clerk. "Mr. Hogarth's only son is the teller of the Bay State Bank in New Jersey. This morning they found that twenty thousand dollars was missing from the vault. No one had access to the vault yesterday but young Hogarth. The cashier was in this city, the combination was not known to any others. There is no evidence of robbery. The circumstances are so overwhelming against young Hogarth that the directors went to him and said plainly that if the money was in its place by Saturday night he would not be prosecuted, and the matter would be hushed up. He protested his innocence, but they simply laughed and would not listen to him. The boy is prostrated, and we know that he is innocent, but there is no way on earth to save him unless Mr. Hogarth can raise the money, which is a hopeless impossibility."

Parks paused, and glanced at Hogarth, the kind of glance that obtains among criminals when they mean, "back up the lie."

The detective buried his face in his hands.

"The discretion of Fate is superb," said Mason. "She strikes always the vulnerable spot. She gives wealth if one does not need it; fame, if one does not care for it; and drives in the harpoon where the heart is."

"The strange thing about it all, sir," continued Parks, "is that Mr. Hogarth has been a detective all his life and now is a member of the Atlantic Agency. It looks like the trailed thing turning on him."

"A detective!" said Mason, sharply. "Ah, there is the open place, and there we will force through."

The whole appearance of the man changed in an instant. He straightened up, and his face lighted with interest. He drew up a chair and sat down at the table, and there, in the chill dark of that November morning, he unfolded the daring details of his cross-plot, and the men beside him stared in wonder.

II.

About one o'clock on Thursday afternoon, William Walson, manager of the great Oceanic Coal Company, stepped out of the Fairmont Banking House in the Monongahela mining regions of West Virginia. It was pay-day at his mine, and he carried a black leather satchel in his hand containing twenty thousand dollars in bills. At this time the gigantic plant of this company was doing an enormous business. The labor unions of the vast Pennsylvania coal regions were out on the bitterest and most protracted strike of all history. The West Virginia operators were moving the heavens in order to supply the market; every man who could hold a pick was at work under the earth day and night.

The excitement was something undreamed of. The region was overrun with straggling workmen, tramps, "hobos," and the scum criminals of the cities, and was transformed as if by magic into a hunting-ground where the keen human ferret stalked the crook and the killer with that high degree of care and patience which obtains only with the man-hunter.

William Walson was tall, with short red beard and red hair, black eyes, and rather a sharp face; his jaw was square, bespeaking energy, but his expression was rather that of a man who won by the milder measures of conciliation and diplomacy. For almost a month he had been taxing his physical strength to the uttermost, and on this afternoon he looked worn and tired out utterly. He walked hurriedly from the bank door to the buck-board, untied the horse, raised the seat, and put the satchel down in the box under the cushion, then climbed in and drove away.

The great plant of the Oceanic Coal Company was on a branch of the railroad, some considerable distance from the main line by rail, but only a few miles over the hills from the Fairmont Junction. William Walson struck out across the country road. The sun shone warm. He had lost so much sleep that presently he began to feel drowsy, and as the horse jogged along he nodded in his seat.

About a mile from the town, at the foot of a little hill in the woods, a man stepped suddenly out from the fence and caught the horse by the bridle. Walson started and looked up. As he did so the stranger covered him with a revolver and bade him put up his hands and get out of the buck-board. The coal dealer saw in a moment that the highwayman meant what he said, and that resistance would be folly. He concluded also that he was confronted by one of the many toughs at large in the neighborhood, and that the fellow's intention was simply to rob him of his personal effects and such money as he might have in his pockets; it was more than probable that the man before him had no knowledge of the money hidden under the seat and would never discover it.

"Tie your horse, sir," said the highwayman.

Walson loosed the hitch strap and fastened the horse to a small tree by the roadside.

"Turn your back to me," said the robber, "and put out your hands behind you." The coal dealer obeyed, thinking that the fellow was now going through his pockets. To his surprise and astonishment the man came up close behind him and snapped a pair of handcuffs on his wrists.

"What do you mean by this?" cried Watson, whirling round on his heels.

The big man with the revolver grinned. "You will find out soon enough," he said. "Move along; the walking is good."

William Watson was utterly at sea. He could not understand why this man should kidnap him, and start back with him to the town. What could the highwayman possibly mean by this queer move? At any rate it was evident that he had no knowledge of the money, and Walson reasoned shrewdly that, if he remained quiet and submissive, the vast sum in the buck-board would escape the notice of this erratic thief.

The two men walked along in silence for some time; the highwayman was big, with keen gray eyes and a shrewd face; he seemed curiously elated. When the two came finally to the brow of the hill overlooking the town, Walson stopped and turned to his strange captor; he was now convinced that the fellow was a lunatic.

"Sir," he said, "what in Heaven's name are you trying to do?"

"Introduce you to your fellows in Sing Sing, my friend," answered the highwayman. "The gang will be glad to welcome Red Lead Jim."

It all came to the coal dealer in a moment "Oh, you miserable ass!" he cried, "what an infernal mistake! My name is William Walson, I am the manager of the Oceanic Coal Company, there is twenty thousand dollars in that buck-board. I must go back to it or it will be lost. Here take off these damned handcuffs, and be quick about it." And he literally danced up and down in the road with rage.

His companion leaned against the fence and roared with laughter. "You are a smooth one, Red, but the job and your twenty thousand will keep."

Walson's face changed. "Come," he said, "let us get this fool business over," and he began to run down the hill to the town, his captor following close beside him.

Men came out into the street in astonishment when they saw the strange pair. Walson was dusty and cursing like a pirate. He called upon the crowd that was quickly gathering, to identify him and arrest his idiotic kidnapper. The people explained that Mr. Walson was all right, that he was a prominent citizen, that it was all some horrible mistake. But the fellow hung on to his man until he got him to the jail. There the sheriff freed Walson and demanded an explanation. The mob crowded around to hear what it all meant. The stranger seemed utterly astonished at the way the people acted. He said that his name was Braxton Hogarth, that he was a New York detective, an employee of the Atlantic Agency; that he was trailing one Red Lead Jim, a famous bank cracker who was wanted in New York for robbery and murder; that he had tracked him to West Virginia, and that coming suddenly upon William Walson in the road he had believed him to be the man, had arrested him, and brought him at once to the town in order to have him extradited. He said that if Walson was not the man it was the most remarkable case of mistaken identity on record. He then produced a photograph, to which was attached a printed description. The photograph was an excellent likeness of Walson, and the description fitted him perfectly. The coal dealer was dumbfounded and joined with the crowd in admitting the excusableness of the detective's mistake under the very peculiar circumstances, but he said that the story might not be true, and asked the sheriff to hold the detective in custody until he was fully convinced that everything was as Hogarth said. The detective declared himself perfectly satisfied with this arrangement, and William Walson secured a horse and hurried back to his buck-board.

The perilous vocation of Hogarth had inured him to tragic positions. He was thoroughly master of his hand and was playing it with quiet and accurate precision. He asked the sheriff to telegraph the agency and inform it of the situation and said that it would immediately establish the truth of his statement.

That night the mining town of Fairmont was in an uproar. The streets were filled with excited men loudly discussing the great misfortune that had so strangely befallen the manager of the Oceanic Coal Company. It had happened that when William Walson returned to his buck-board, after his release by the sheriff, he found the horse lying dead by the roadside, and the buck-board a heap of ashes and broken irons. The charred remains of the satchel were found under the heap of rubbish, but it was impossible to determine whether the money had been carried away or destroyed by the fire. A jug that had lately contained liquor was found near by. All the circumstances indicated that the atrocious act was the malicious work of some one of the roving bands of drunken cutthroats. But the wonder of it all was the coincidence of the detective and the glaring boldness of the fiend "hobos."

The Atlantic Agency of New York, answered the sheriff's telegram immediately, confirming Hogarth's statement, and referring to the District Attorney of New York and the Chief of Police; These answered that the agency was all right and that its statement should be accepted as correct. Finally, as a last precaution, the sheriff and the president of the Oceanic Coal Company talked with the New York Police Chief by long-distance telephone. When they were at length assured that the detective's story was true, he was released and asked to go with the president before the board of directors. Here he went fully over the whole matter, explaining that the man, Red Lead Jim, was a desperate character, and for that reason he had been so severe and careful, not daring to risk the drive back to town in the buck-board. When asked his theory of the robbery, he said that the first impression of the people was undoubtedly correct, that the country was full of wandering gangs of desperate blacklegs, that the money being in paper was perhaps destroyed by the fire and not discovered at all by the thugs in their malicious and drunken deviltry.

The board of directors were not inclined to censure Hogarth, suggesting that after all he had perhaps saved the life of William Walson, as it was evident that the drunken "hobos" would have murdered him if he had been present when they chanced upon the horse and buck-board. Nevertheless, the detective seemed utterly prostrated over the great loss that had resulted from his unfortunate mistake, and left for New York on the first train.

III.

The following night two men stepped from the train at Jersey City and turned down towards the ferry. For a time they walked along in silence; suddenly the big one turned to his companion. "Parks," he said, "you are a lightning operator, my boy, you should play the mob in a Roman drama."

"I fixed the 'hobo' evidence all right, Hogarth," answered the other, "and I have not forgotten the trust fund," whereupon he winked at his big companion and tapped on the breast of his coat significantly.

The detective's face lighted up and then grew anxious. "Well," he said, lowering his voice, "are we going to try the other end of it?"

"Why not?" answered the little clerk. "Don't we need the trust fund doubled?"

IV.

The great gambling house of Morehead, Opstein, & Company was beginning to be deserted by the crowd that had tempted the fickle goddess all night long to their great hurt. It was now four o'clock in the morning, and only one or two of the more desperate losers hung on to play. Snakey the Parson, a thin delicate knave, with a long innocent, melancholy face, was dealing faro for the house. "Snakey" was a "special" in the parlance of the guild; his luck was known to come in "blizzards"; if he won, to use the manager's language, he won out through the ceiling, and if he lost, he lost down to his health. For this reason Snakey the Parson was not a safe man as a "regular," but he was a golden bonanza when the cards went his way, and to-night they were going his way.

The stragglers drifted out one by one and the dealer was preparing to quit the table when the door opened and two men entered: one was a little old man with a white beard and a lean, hungry face; the other was a big, half-drunken cattle drover. The two came up to the table and stood for a moment looking at the lay-out. A faint smile passed over the face of Snakey the Parson, he knew the types well, they were western cattle-shippers with money.

"How high do ye go, mister?" said the little man.

"Against the sky," answered the dealer, sadly.

"Then I'll jist double me pile," said the little old man, reaching down into his pocket and fishing up a roll of bills wrapped in a dirty old newspaper. He counted the money and placed it upon the table.

The dealer looked up in astonishment. "Ten thousand!" he said.

"Yep," answered the old man, "an I want ter bet hit on the jack er spades."

The dealer pushed a stack of yellow chips across the table.

"No, siree," said the player, "you don't give me no buttons. I' ll put my pile on this side and you put your pile on t'other side, and the winner takes 'em."

Snakey the Parson wavered a moment. It was against the rules, but here was too good a thing to lose. He turned, counted out the money, and placed it on his right, and began to deal from the box. The cards fell rapidly. For a time the blacks ran on the side of the house. Suddenly they changed and the queen and the ten of spades fell on the left. The dealer saw the card under his thumb and paused. The keen eyes of the old man were fixed on him. He determined to take the long chance, knowing that the loss was only temporary; and the jack of spades came up and fell on the side of the stranger.

With a whoop of joy the old man clutched the money. "I am going to try her agin!" he cried.

"Hold on," said the big cattle-drover, pushing up to the table; "my wad is as good as you; it is my turn now."

The dealer grinned. "You can both play, gentlemen," he said, speaking with a low, sweet accent.

"No, we can't," muttered the drover, with the childish obstinacy of a half-drunken man. "I want the whole shooting match to myself; he can have the next whirl at her."

Thereupon the drover dragged a big red pocket book from somewhere inside his coat, took out a thick, straight package of bills, and laid it down on the table.

"How much?" said the dealer, running his finger over the end of the package.

"'Same as Abe's," said the drover.

"Here," said the little old man, peevishly, "if you won't let me play, bet my roll with yourn," and he pushed the ten thousand of his own money to his companion, and placed the money, which he had won from the bank, in his pocket. The drover took the money and piled it up on the ace of spades.

The dealer's face grew pensive and sweet; it was all right this time; he was going to round off the night with a golden *coup d' état*. He opened the safe behind him, counted out twenty thousand in big bills, and piled it up on one side of the bank. Then he opened the box and began. The old man wandered around the room; the big, half-drunken cattle-shipper hung over the table. Snakey, the Parson scarcely saw either; he was intent on manipulating the box, and his hand darted in and out like a white snake. Suddenly the ace of spades flew out, and fell on the side of the house. The quick dealer clapped his left hand over the box and put out his right for the player's money. As he did so, the big drover bent forward and thrust a revolver into his face.

"No, you don't," he growled, "this is my money and I will not leave it, thank you."

Snakey the Parson glanced at the man and knew that he had been fooled, but he was composed and clear-headed. Under the box on the right were weapons and the electric button; he began to take his right hand slowly from the table.

"Stop!" said the drover, sharply, "that game won't work!"

The dealer looked up into the player's face, and dropped his hands; he was a brave man, and desperate, as gamblers go, but he knew death when he saw it; his face turned yellow and became ghastly, but he did not move.

The drover took up his money from the lay-out, and handed it to the old man. He used his left hand only, and did not take his eyes from the gambler's face. The old man thrust the bundle of bills in his pocket, and hurried from the room. The gambler sat rigid as a wax figure. The drover waited until his companion had sufficient time to get thoroughly away from the house; then he began to move slowly backward to the door, keeping the gambler covered with the weapon. The faro dealer watched every move of the drover, like a hawk, but he did not attempt to take his hand from the table; the muzzle of the revolver was too rigid; it was simply moving backward from his face in a dead straight line. At the door the drover stopped, drew himself together, then sprang suddenly through and bounded down the stairs.

Snakey the Parson touched the electric button, and as the drover rushed into the street, two policemen caught him by the shoulder.

V

Well," said the Police Chief, "I am tired of making an ass of myself; Mr. Mason says this cattle drover has committed no crime except a petty assault, and if he is right, I want to know it. That man beats the very devil. Every time I have sent up a case against his protest the judges have pitched me out on my neck, and the thing has got to be cursedly monotonous."

The District Attorney smiled grimly, and turned around in his chair. "Have you given me all the details?" he said.

"Yes," answered the official, "just exactly as they occurred."

The District Attorney arose, thrust his hands into his pockets, and looked down at the great man-hunter; there was a queer set to his mouth, and the merest shadow of a twinkle in his eyes.

"Well, my friend," he said, "you are pitched out on your neck again."

The official drew a deep breath, and his face fell. "Then it is not robbery?" he said.

"No," answered the attorney.

"Well," mused the Police Chief, "this law business is too high for me. I have spent my life dealing with crimes, and I thought I knew one when I saw it; but I give it up, I don't know the first principles. Why, here is a fellow who voluntarily goes into a gambling house, plays and loses, then draws a revolver and forcibly takes away the money which, by the rules of the play, belongs to the house; robs the dealer by threatening to kill him; steals the bank's money, and fights his way out. It cannot matter that the man robbed was a lawbreaker himself, or that the crime occurred in a gambling house. It is the law of New York that has been violated; the place and parties are of no importance. Here is certainly the force and the putting in fear that constitute the vital element of robbery; and yet you say it is not robbery. You have me lost all right."

"My dear sir," put in the District Attorney, "the vital element of robbery is not the force and terror but is what is called in the books the *animus furandi*, meaning the intention to steal. The presence of this felonious intent determines whether or not the wrong is a crime. If it be not present there can be no robbery, no matter how great the force, violence, or putting in fear, or how graven serious, or irreparable the resulting injury.

"It is true indeed that the force and terror are elements, but the vital one is the intent. If force and violence one takes his own property from the possession of another, it is no robbery; nor is it robbery for one to take the property of another by violence under the belief that it is his own, or that he has some right to it, or by mistake or misunderstanding, although vast loss be caused thereby and great wrong and hurt result."

"I have no hope of ever understanding it," said the Police Chief; "I am only a common man with a short life time."

"Why, sir," continued the attorney, "it is as plain as sunlight. Robbery is compounded of larceny and force. It is larceny from the person by violence, but in order to constitute it the property must be taken from the peaceable possession of the party and it must be taken *animo furandi*. Neither of these happened in the case you state, because the faro dealer, by means of an unlawful game, could not secure any color of right or title to the money which he should win by it. Therefore the money taken was not his property, and could not have been taken from his peaceable possession.

"In the second place, this vital element of robbery, the animus furandi, is totally wanting, for the reason that the player, in forcibly seizing the money which he had lost, was actuated by no intention to steal, but, on the contrary, was simply taking possession of his own property, property to which he had a full legal right and title."

"But," put in the officer, "there was the other ten thousand which the old man won, they got away with that; if the game was unlawful they had no right to that."

"True," said the lawyer. "The old man had no title to the ten thousand which he had won, but he did not steal it; the dealer gave it to him of his own free will, and the old man had it in his possession by the full voluntary consent of the dealer some time before the resort to violence. There was clearly no crime in this."

"Damn it all!" said the Police Chief, wearily, "is there no way to get at him, can't we railroad him before a jury?"

The District Attorney looked at the baffled officer and grinned ominously. "My friend," he said, "there is no power in Venice can alter a decree established. The courts have time and again passed upon cases exactly similar to this, and have held that there was no crime, except, perhaps, a petty misdemeanor. We could not weather a proceeding on *habeas corpus* ten minutes; we could never get to a jury. When the judge came to examine the decisions on this question we would go out, as you expressed it, on our necks."

"Well," muttered the Police Chief, as he pulled on his coat, "it is just as Randolph Mason said, out he goes."

The attorney laughed and turned to his desk. The officer crossed to the door, jerked it open, then stopped and faced round. "Mr. District Attorney," he said, "won't there be hell to pay when the crooks learn the law?" Then he stalked through and banged the door after him.

The District Attorney looked out of the window and across the street at the dirty row of ugly buildings. "Humph!" he said, "there is something in that last remark of the Chief."

VI.

Braxton Hogarth, detective, member of the Atlantic Agency, in good standing, now, by right of law and by virtue of his craft, restored to his freedom and identity, stepped back and was swallowed up by the crowd.

The great ocean liner steamed out from the port of New York on its pathless journey to the sunny south of France. Randolph Mason sat in an invalid chair close up to the rail of the deck; he was grim, emaciated, and rigidly ugly. His body was exhausted, worn out utterly long ago, but the fierce mysterious spirit of the man was tireless and wrought on unceasingly.

For a time he was silent, his eyes wide, and his jaw set like a wolf trap. Suddenly he clutched the rail and staggered to his feet.

"Parks," he muttered,—"Parks, this ship is worth a million dollars. Come with me to the cabin and I will show you how it may be wrested from the owners and no crime committed; do you understand me, Parks? no crime!"

Note.—For the purpose of a complete demonstration, two situations are here combined. In the first, the crime of robbery was committed, but in such a manner as to completely evade an inference of the animus furandi*, although it was in fact present and obtained. In the second, there was no robbery, the* animus furandi *being entirely absent, although it apparently existed in a conspicuous degree.*

THE END.